Also by Will H. Theus

Savannah Furniture, 1735–1825

How to Collect and Detect Antique Furniture

How to
Detect and Collect
Antique Porcelain
and
Pottery

WILL H. THEUS

How to
Detect and Collect
Antique Porcelain
and
Pottery

ALFRED A. KNOPF   NEW YORK
1974

THIS IS A BORZOI BOOK
PUBLISHED BY ALFRED A. KNOPF, INC.

Copyright © 1974 by Will H. Theus
All rights reserved under International and
Pan-American Copyright Conventions.
Published in the United States by Alfred A. Knopf, Inc., New York,
and simultaneously in Canada by Random House
of Canada Limited, Toronto.
Distributed by Random House, Inc., New York.

Library of Congress Cataloging in Publication Data:

Theus, Will H., date.
How to detect and collect antique porcelain and pottery.

Bibliography: p.
1. Porcelain—Collectors and collecting.
2. Pottery—Collectors and collecting. I. Title.
NK4230.T48   738'.075   74-7747
ISBN 0-394-49130-0
ISBN 0-394-70984-5 (pbk.)

First Edition
Manufactured in the United States of America

To my grandchildren:
Anne, Emerson, Charlton,
and Charlotte

Contents

Color Plates

Text Illustrations

Photographs are by Louis Schwartz of Charleston, S.C.,
with the exceptions of the ones of the Meissen platter,
Leeds chestnut bowl, Leeds coffeepots, and Rookwood vase,
which are by Beth Lattimore of Savannah, Ga.

Acknowledgments

The illustrations in this book are of objects generally available to the beginning collector, and not of ones from museum collections. Grateful acknowledgment goes to the following people who generously lent me porcelain and pottery to be photographed: Mr. Harlyn Dickinson; Mr. and Mrs. Walter Dowling; Mrs. Alida Harper Fowlkes; Miss Isabelle Harrison; Mrs. Stewart Huston; Mrs. Ralston B. Lattimore; Carl Meadows, Inc., Antiques, Savannah, Georgia; Mr. Dean Owens, Nathaniel Russell House, Charleston, South Carolina; Mr. and Mrs. George E. Quaile; The Red Torii, Charleston; Schindler's Antique Shop, Charleston; Peter Schwerin, Colonial Antique Shop, Charleston; and Mrs. Don C. Sharp, Jr., Allendale, S.C.

Special appreciation is extended to Miss Beth Lattimore, Assistant Director, Historic Savannah Foundation Incorporated, Savannah, and to Mrs. William F. Summerell, my typist.

The photographs are by Louis Schwartz, Charleston, and the sketches by Mrs. George E. Quaile.

W. H. T.

Isle of Hope, Savannah, Georgia
April 1974

How to
Detect and Collect
Antique Porcelain
and
Pottery

I

Notes
for the Beginner

Antique shops and antique shows, junk shops, and garage sales are attracting more and more people and buyers every year. Many people are inclined to think they can pick up a bargain because the seller doesn't know what he has. This is seldom true, but when it does happen it gives the buyer enormous satisfaction.

Probably the most sought-for items are porcelain and pottery. One reason for this is that people know that an item such as a plate or a cup can be fitted into their living quarters no matter how small. Often with this in mind, a collection is started.

What should you collect? Anything you might desire or

that catches your fancy. A weakness for cats, horses, dogs, pigs, sheep, or shells may spur you on to look for figures in your special category or for dishes illustrating them. You might want to fill out a pattern of china that was left to you or, more ambitiously, collect items from a certain Continental factory. In any case, whatever you choose to collect, acquire articles of quality and of good design no matter what the age. Choose something that you can continue to live with or sell advantageously. Keep in mind that it is not the quantity of the collection that counts but the quality.

You may ask, "What about a damaged piece?" It depends on the scarcity or rarity of the article. If it is a type or shape that is scarce and you want a particular example, do not hesitate to buy a damaged piece. But remember that a damaged or restored piece should cost much less than an article of the same in perfect, or proof, condition.

Antique ceramics may be approached aesthetically and collected with a view to showing the development of decorative art in each country. A scientific student of history cannot afford to ignore the detailed study of social conditions pictured by ceramic articles. The development of costume, of furniture, and of the domestic arts portrayed on the articles gives life and color to written history records, and porcelain and pottery may be collected as an adjunct to furniture by those who prefer to see several phases of art harmonized in a scheme of decoration.

The ordinary person finds an absorbing hobby in the collection of porcelain and pottery. He reads of the prices that remarkable specimens bring at auction, and he begins to think that his education has been partly neglected, since he knows little or nothing about these art treasures that attract others. "Collecting for profit" is a phrase that is beguiling, and many "collectors" regard their purchases solely as investments. Don't fall into this trap, or you will miss the pleasure of owning a piece for its sheer beauty and appeal. The "china shelf" is now regarded as worthy of discriminating study. Treasures, often heirlooms, are brought to light, and amateur collectors can be numbered in the thousands.

It is my hope that the following chapters on collecting antique porcelain and pottery, a mere outline of the subject for the beginner or novice, may point the way to a better appreciation of what is really of value in this field and may help to identify questionable pieces.

It is impossible in this abbreviated primer to cover all kinds of porcelain and pottery. I have purposely omitted articles that are not found in any quantity in American shops, such as Italian and Russian pieces and products of lesser factories. I have also not mentioned Japanese ceramics, since they continue to be made and exported in such vast quantities as to make Japanese porcelain and pottery a subject all its own.

This book *does* include the various types of ceramics—porcelain, pottery, stoneware, delft, etc.—and does include Chinese and Chinese Export ceramics, as well as the output of the major factories of Germany, Austria, France, England, and America. Reference to many other factories and porcelain makers, along with unfamiliar terms, may be found in the Glossary. It is impossible to give specific prices since they fluctuate continually according to the scarcity of the article and its current popularity, but the porcelain and pottery considered here were selected with their availability to the "average" buyer in mind.

II

Identifying Porcelain and Pottery

The potential collector must handle as many articles as possible to get the feel, the actual tactile sensation, of porcelain and pottery. No matter how many books you read, pictures you see, or articles you observe in museums and private collections, nothing can contribute as much to your knowledge as touching and holding the articles. The physical property that makes pieces different to the touch is the plasticity of the clay, whether they are thrown on the wheel, which is peculiar to the art of the potter, or modelled, molded, or cast, which is shared with other arts. Clays and conditions of firing vary, and with the variety of material

Porcelain and pottery bowls, both in underglaze blue.
The porcelain bowl was made by William Ratcliff,
Hanley, c. 1830, and the Historic Staffordshire pottery bowl
of Hartford Courthouse was made c. 1825 by an unknown potter.
It is hard to tell much about the bowls without being able
to check for translucence or actually handling them, although
even in the photograph the gloss of the glaze gives a hint.

comes a wide range of purely sensuous appeal. Texture may range from the coarse earthenware of ancient times to the soft porcelain of Sèvres.

Many factors must be considered in identifying articles. First you must decide what the object is—porcelain or pottery. The easiest and most general test is to hold it up to a strong light. If you can see light through it—if it is translucent—that signifies that it is porcelain or china, two words describing the same thing. There are exceptions: If the porcelain is in a particularly heavy mass, such as might be found at the base of figures, you will not be able to see through it. Also, some porcelains are not as translucent as others, because the amounts of the ingredients in the paste vary, as well as temperatures at which they were fired. Even in these exceptions, there is usually some degree of translucence where the body is at all thin, such as at the edges of plates and saucers, or lips and moldings.

In addition to translucence, the quality that differentiates porcelain from other ceramic products is the whiteness of its body, not merely on the surface but clean through the substance, as can be seen when it is broken. There are other qualities, less dependable for identification, but perhaps useful in conjunction with the first two. One is that when the edge of a porcelain bowl or plate is struck, it will give forth a clear, bell-like note. There is also a distinctive manner in which porcelain glaze reflects the light, and to the touch the surface is as smooth and soft as mother-of-pearl.

If light cannot be seen through an object—if it is opaque —that means it is a piece of pottery or earthenware, synonymous words. Pottery includes rare earthenware bowls and figures from the T'ang and Sung dynasties; various tin-glazed earthenwares, which are termed, according to country, faience, majolica, and delft; English salt-glazed enamel articles; and Wedgwood's classical jasper urns. Although the ordinary clay flowerpot is also in this category, there is much pottery and earthenware that is considered fine art.

It should be mentioned here that some stoneware, a hard paste pottery, has some of the same characteristics as porcelain—the hardness of hard paste porcelain, whiteness, and even on occasions a slight translucence. Contrary to most earthenwares, which need a coating of glaze to protect their porous defects, stoneware has a hard body needing none. Frequently stoneware is found glazed, and when it is, the glaze is usually a salt glaze.

III

Historical Background

Pottery goes back to the beginning of time; the making of it is one of the oldest branches of human industry. It sprang from the obvious need for containers. Early people must have observed that the falling of rain upon the earth would soften it and render it malleable, while the influence of the sun and air would dry and harden it. It was a natural progression to fashion the soft clay into rude cups and bowls and to dry them in the heat of the sun.

Porcelain is a comparatively modern achievement dating from the T'ang Dynasty (A.D. 618–906). The earliest surviving piece, however, is from the Sung Dynasty (A.D. 960–1267). Porcelain may have been first brought into Europe by the Moors, or by the Crusaders, who found it in the Near East at the end of the Chinese trade routes.

Marco Polo, who travelled in Asia between 1271 and 1295 and spent twenty years at the court of Kublai Khan, Emperor of China, is said to have brought back a small white vase of Ying-ch'ing ware when he returned to Venice. However, Europe's real concern with Oriental porcelain dates from the fifteenth century. In 1447, according to Matheur du Coussy, the historian of Charles VII, King of France, a letter addressed to the Sultan of Babylon concludes with a request for a present of porcelain to be conveyed to the King of France by his ambassador. And after 1498, when the sea route to India was opened by Vasco da Gama's voyage around the Cape of Good Hope, porcelain began to be brought to the West regularly, although the number of objects was still relatively small. During the sixteenth century, whenever a piece did find its way to Europe, it was so highly prized that it was usually set in silver or gold.

It was not until the European nations sent ships to the East and established the well-organized trading companies, generally known as East India companies, that the trade assumed serious proportions. The Portuguese reached China first in 1516, and about 1536 they founded a trading post, or factory (an expression meaning a place of residence of the factors or the company), at Macao, a tiny settlement on a promontory at the mouth of the Canton River. In 1599 the English established their East India Company, which was destined to become the most powerful of all and was to be influential in establishing England's far-flung empire. English ships visited Canton for the first time in 1631.

The Dutch East India Company set up its operations in Canton in 1602 and almost immediately began to import vast amounts of blue-and-white porcelain. In the period

1604 to 1657, it is estimated that at least three million porcelains came to Dutch ports. In 1604 one hundred thousand pieces of porcelain, captured from the ship *Catharina*, were auctioned at Amsterdam. Buyers came from all over Western Europe, including Henry IV of France and King James of England, who acquired large dinner sets.

China mania became an epidemic that held the whole of Europe enthralled. That this translucent ware had travelled safely the long journey from the Far East astonished European potters. They had no idea how it was made. The French called it "porcelaine" from the cowrie shell, which had the same mother-of-pearl luster. Because it was imported from China, the English called it "china-ware." It provoked wide imitation. The new habit of tea and coffee drinking in the middle of the seventeenth century added further to its popularity. There were many collectors—from Queen Mary, wife of William III, who was an avid buyer and admirer of porcelain, to Mistress Nell Gwynne, who went down to the docks and poked through the cargoes of newly arrived East Indiamen in order that she might have the first pick of anything that pleased her fancy. With such interest abounding throughout Europe, it was only natural that the potters of each country try to produce facsimiles of this translucent ware of the East. In many cases the ruling classes were behind these efforts in the hope of gaining riches. The first porcelain made in Europe was in Florence, where after other unsuccessful attempts, a soft paste (not the true hard paste of China) called Medici porcelain was made in the late sixteenth century. This venture was begun in 1575 by Francesco I de' Medici, Grand Duke of Tuscany, and ended with his death in 1587. Only about seventy-two pieces of this early ceramic are extant.

France was producing a soft paste porcelain by 1673 at Rouen. The first hard paste porcelain, or true porcelain, like that being brought in from China, was produced at

Meissen in 1715, when Augustus II (Augustus the Strong), King of Poland and Elector of Saxony, established a factory on the Elbe about twelve miles from Dresden, for the manufacturing of hard paste, or true, porcelain. Long before Augustus the Strong acceded to the electoral throne of Saxony and was made King of Poland (a crown he acquired at auction in 1696), he became an insatiable collector of Chinese porcelain. He thought that his extraordinary collection would contribute to his esteem and guarantee his eventual election as Emperor of the Holy Empire. Although disappointed in that, he did have the satisfaction of being the first European ruler to possess a porcelain factory of his own and the first to produce a hard paste porcelain in Europe. The credit for the duplication of hard paste belongs to Johann Friedrich Böttger, an alchemist. The King of Prussia had heard that a subject was able to transmute the base metals into gold and planned to seize him. Böttger learned of the plot and fled to Saxony. Augustus the Strong was quite as much in need of funds as the King of Prussia, and here was a "gold maker" fallen into his very lap. He seized Böttger and set him to work to make gold, which of course ended in failure; but someone suggested to the King that he use the apparatus for a faience factory instead.

The subsequent history of this factory reads like a fairy story. At first, hard redware like jasper was made, but soon Böttger, still in the service of Augustus, discovered by accident the Chinese principle of combining an infusible white clay, kaolin, with a fusible mineral substance. After this, Augustus held the workers in the factory prisoners so that they would not be able to reveal the secret.

Ownership of a porcelain factory soon became an essential attribute of the magnificence and dignity of any ruling prince. Thus, it was not surprising that despite all precautions the secret found its way to Vienna in 1719, where the second porcelain factory was established. In October 1717, after unsuccessful experiments in the manufacture of porcelain, Claudius Innocentius du Pacquier persuaded Christoph Konrad Hunger to desert from Meissen to Vienna. Hunger claimed to have received the secrets of the making of hard paste porcelain from Böttger.

This was just the beginning. By the middle of the eighteenth century a string of hard paste porcelain factories had sprung up: at Höchst by 1746, at Nymphenburg and Fürstenburg by 1747. The great royal and national porcelain factory of Sèvres started producing a soft paste ware at Vincennes in 1738, and moved to Sèvres in 1756, although it was not until about 1766 that the directors of the Sèvres factory purchased the secret for hard paste porcelain.

In England soft paste porcelain was being made before 1750 at Chelsea, Bow, and Worcester. Many other factories soon followed. A totally independent reinvention of hard paste porcelain was achieved by William Cookworthy of Plymouth in 1768, too late to capture any significant place in the European market. It is probable that in undeveloped America, Andrew Duché, of Savannah, accomplished as much by 1738. It is claimed he was the first English-speaking person to produce true porcelain. When he failed to get financial help from the Trustees of Savannah, he went to London in 1744 and contacted English potters hoping to interest them in the manufacture of true porcelain. It is thought that it was through him that Cookworthy learned the formula for true porcelain.

IV

Five Important Facts
to Keep in Mind

After determining if an article is porcelain or pottery, there are five factors to keep in mind in identifying an article of ceramics:

1. Paste
2. Glaze
3. Decoration
4. Contour, or shape
5. Mark

Paste

Paste is the mixture of clay and other materials of which the body of the article is composed. Pottery is either soft

or hard paste, depending on how it is fired. Soft paste
pottery is a mixture of clay and other mineral substances
fired to a hardness sufficient for practical use but still re-
maining porous and unable to hold fluids unless covered
by a glaze. Firing earthenware harder than usual produces
an incipient fusion of the mass that renders it impervious
to liquids. Some examples of hard paste pottery (or stoneware) are the fine redwares, black basalts, and jasper.

Porcelain may be hard paste, soft paste, or bone. The
porcelain that was imported from China and imitated by
the Europeans was a true, or hard paste, porcelain. It is
made from a mixture of china clay (kaolin) and china
rock (petuntse), is resistant to a file, and shows a con-
choidal, or shell-like, fracture. Hard paste porcelain is glazed
with a preparation of petuntse, and the body and the glaze
are fired at an extremely high temperature, 1350 to 1500
degrees centigrade.

Expressed in the simplest terms, soft paste, or artificial,
porcelain was ground glass stiffened with white clay to give
the mixture stability. It can be marked by a file, and when
chipped it can be seen that the body is granular. It must
be fired before glazing to set the soft body. Soft paste porcelain is difficult to fire successfully, since the temperature
range, 1100 to 1150 degrees centigrade, is extremely narrow
and difficult to maintain. Comparatively minor variations
upward or downward often spoil the entire contents of the
kiln. After the initial firing further firings at successively
lower temperatures of about 1000 degrees are necessary to
set the glaze, the overglaze enamel decoration, and gilding
when used. The soft paste body was improved from time to
time by the addition of other substances, notably soapstone,
bone ash, and feldspar. When fired it has a soft, soapy
surface to the touch, less dense than hard paste, yet translucent and granular. Since it is porous, an unglazed soft
paste base absorbs dirt and cannot be scrubbed clean.

Bone china was an early nineteenth-century hybrid porcelain, mixing the white ash of calcined bones (a characteristic of English soft paste) with the ingredients of hard paste. This produced the strength of hard paste with the softness and beauty of soft paste. Bone china was first marketed by Josiah Spode in 1794. His formula is the standard to this day: bone ash, 6 parts; china (Cornish) clay, 3½ parts; and china stone, 4 parts. It is fired in a very high temperature oven, about 1500 degrees.

Examples of hard paste porcelains are: Chinese, Chinese Export, the output of the Meissen and other German factories, and practically all Continental porcelain, with the exception of the early French wares. All English porcelain, with the exception of Plymouth, Bristol, and New Hall, for a short time, was of soft paste until the early nineteenth century, when the formula for bone china was adopted by most factories.

Glaze

Glaze is another form of the word glass, and there is not a great deal of difference between the chemical composition of the glaze on the surface of china and glass. When a piece is unglazed, such as in some medallions and busts, it is spoken of as "in the biscuit," or bisque.

The application of a glassy material to ceramics renders them impervious to liquids and smooth to the touch. Glaze may be dull, mat, shiny translucent, or opaque, or it may be shot through with brilliant color. Glaze may be hard and resistant to a knife edge, or it may be soft and easily scratched. Glaze is usually transparent and almost colorless. The exceptions in porcelain are the Oriental colored glazes, which appear on some of the finest and rarest wares. These include celadon, blue, yellow, black, purple, and

The side and base views of this First Period
Worcester bowl illustrate important factors to look for
in identifying a ceramic article: the underglaze base is porous
and has absorbed dirt, indicating a soft paste body;

and the reticulated, or fretwork, rim—with its molded,
applied flowers—and the underglaze-blue decoration
help point to date and factory. The mark, here a blue crescent,
confirms an already fairly definite attribution. C. 1765.

red.· In China the glaze was made of the pure petuntse, or china stone, sometimes softened with a little lime, and was applied in a thin fluid state to the air-dried but still unfired objects. The colored glazes were achieved by the addition of oxidized metallic pigments, such as cobalt (blue), iron (celadon greens and yellow or buff color), copper (red), and manganese (black and purple).

Colored glazes were rarely used on porcelain on the Continent and in England, but they were used on earthenware. Many cream-colored earthenwares were enriched with semi-translucent colored glazes. The ware known as "tortoise shell" is decorated with mottled patterns in blue, green, and brown tints derived from the oxides of cobalt, copper, and manganese. Most commercial earthenware factories of the 1740–1780 period produced this type of ware. Mid-nineteenth-century English "majolica," emulating the early Italian majolica, was earthenware covered with a semi-translucent colored glaze.

Lead glaze, the commonest form of pottery glaze, was composed of silica in the form of sand or quartz fused with the aid of a flux such as potash, lime, or soda and oxide of lead. This was applied by dusting the powdered ore on the ware before firing. Lead glaze was in general use from early times until the end of the nineteenth century, but it was very detrimental to the health of the potters. John Rose invented a leadless glaze for porcelain in 1820, which was awarded the Isis Gold Medal of the Society of Arts, and Job Meigh invented a leadless glaze for red earthenware in 1822.

A salt glaze was often used and was achieved by throwing salt into an intensely hot kiln; the resulting vapor deposited a fine layer of glaze on the stoneware, which gave it a texture similar to orange peel. This technique developed by 1680.

In their attempt to ape the Chinese blue-and-white porcelain, the Dutch dipped or covered natural-colored clay pottery in a glaze of oxide of tin to make it white and opaque. A product of this method is called tin-glazed enamel, the glaze used on the well-known delft ware.

Decoration

Porcelain and pottery may be decorated in two ways. First the decoration may be contained in the body of the piece itself and consist of engraving, embossing, perforations or fret-work, or applied reliefs. All these devices are perfected before glazing. This is called decoration in the white. Second, the decoration may be accomplished by colors or gilding.

Decoration in the white is effected by engraving or incising patterns in the body of the article before it is fired, or the patterns may be impressed by the mold in which the article is first shaped. When patterns are embossed in low relief, they are made by the molds, or, when higher relief is desired, patterns are produced by painting with thickslip (a form of clay) upon the surface of the air-dried article. When the slip painting has dried, the article is ready for glazing and firing. Occasionally the article is first covered with a colored glaze and fired, and then painted with white slip. This necessitates a second glazing and firing. Examples of the low embossed or raised patterns are to be found in the basketwork now and again occurring on the rims of plates or bowls. Perforations or fretwork, such as that on plate rims and in fruit baskets, are often a distinctive decoration. Separately molded reliefs—such as rosettes for the intersections of fretwork, sprigs, flowers, and the various sorts of figures used as knobs and handles—were attached with slip to the body of the piece before glazing.

The colors used in decorating ceramics are of two sorts:

the underglaze colors, those applied before glazing and firing, and the enamel colors and gold applied after glazing, or so-called overglaze decoration. These enamel colors and gold require a second firing in a muffle kiln (an oven used in a furnace to protect the article from the flame) at the comparatively low temperature of 700 degrees centigrade, to make them fuse with the glaze and become permanent. The most substantial and reliable underglaze color is blue, made from cobalt, which explains the reason for the early Chinese blue-and-white porcelain, and later the underglaze blue in early Continental and English wares.

The overglaze enamels were easy to use and produced varied effects. Enamel colors on the glaze of hard paste porcelain often stand up perceptibly from the surface of the glaze. The glaze is so hard that the enamel colors, which require a comparatively low temperature for their firing, do not thoroughly fuse with it. On the other hand, enamel colors applied over the glaze of soft paste porcelain very often melt into and become incorporated with it so that their presence above the surface of the glaze is neither visible to the eye nor noticeable by touch. A third way of applying color decoration is by the use of colored glazes, explained on page 20. Other types of decorations are gilding, transfer printing, and luster.

Gold has been used as a decoration on ceramics for centuries. Several methods of applying it to ceramic surfaces were adopted in the eighteenth century: size gilding, lacquer gilding, honey gilding, and mercury gilding.

Size gilding consisted of applying leaf gold to decorations painted in gold size when it had partly dried and become tacky. It was usual on Italian majolica and some early faience, as well as on English soft paste porcelains, such as those of Bow and Longton Hall. Size gilding did not stand up well to everyday use. Lacquer gilding was painting with gold leaf ground up in a lacquer solution and was used in Böttger's redware. Honey gilding was a more satisfactory process that used a mixture of gold leaf ground up in a honey solution, which was subsequently lightly fired. It produced a soft, dull tone of considerable beauty and provided the chance to paint the decorations with a sufficient weight of gold to withstand subsequent chasing and tooling. Mercury gilding began about 1780 and consisted of a gold-and-mercury mixture that could be painted onto the ware, the mercury being driven off as a vapor during the firing process. Subsequently the gold was burnished with an agate to great brilliance. This is generally much showier but less attractive.

A bright but slightly brassy-looking liquid gold that did not need burnishing after firing was introduced in the nineteenth century. It does not compare with the rich, dull gold used previously.

In transfer printing, a design was etched onto a piece of copper, and while the copper was still hot, the ceramic color was rubbed into it. A spatula was used to remove the excess paint and make it smooth, and the copper was then carefully wiped with a clean cloth. Wet tissue was then placed on the hot copper, and the whole put between rollers. The tissue was peeled off, having received a reverse print of the ceramic color, and was pressed with a sticky substance onto the object to receive the design. This process, which was discovered about 1753, was repeated on each article to be so decorated. At first it was done over the glaze but later under the glaze when it was discovered what colors could be used in that way.

The process of luster decoration originated with Hispano-Moresque and Italian pottery and consists of a layer of pigments, containing sulphides of copper or silver, that is painted over the glaze, previously fixed. For all practical purposes English lusterware is divided into three groups: copper or brown, purple or gold, silver or platinum. Pieces are also designated by the ground shades; for example, canary or apricot luster. Copper luster was the first made, beginning around 1770; the best copper luster was made about 1801. Among the metallic luster decorations silver is perhaps the most highly prized. It contained no silver; the effect was produced by an oxide of platinum, thinly applied with a brush. In addition to silver luster, there was silver "resist." After the article was glazed, a design was penciled or painted on it in an adhesive mixture—glycerine, treacle, or shellac. The article was then dipped in a bath of platinum and completely coated except for the decoration, which "resisted" the metallic solution.

All these types of decoration were used singly or in combination. They can help in determining the date and at times the place of manufacture.

Contour, or Shape

The shape, or contour, of an object is always a clue to its identification. It is obvious that a piece could not have been made before any particular style was in vogue; on the other hand, a shape of an early date may enjoy permanent favor. The following style periods do not describe ceramics alone but include painting, architecture, and furniture as well. Characteristic contours and approximate dates are:

BAROQUE: seventeenth century and the early years of the eighteenth century. It is a dramatic style, and one with unusual, irregular, and grotesque forms. Much of the decorative art of Germany and Austria is baroque, and it is seen in the early porcelain of Meissen and Vienna.

ROCOCO: first half of the eighteenth century. A florid style of ornamentation characterized by C-, double C-, and S-curved lines, and decoration of pierced shellwork.

NEO-CLASSIC: middle and late eighteenth century. As its name implies, it is a return to the characteristics of ancient Greece and Rome. The use of swags, urns, and plaited cable ornament is common. In England it was introduced by Robert Adam, who had spent four years in Italy and Dalmatia making excavations of Classic ruins. Perhaps the greatest ceramic exponent was Josiah Wedgwood. The pastel colors of his jasper were inspired by the palette adopted for mural and ceiling decoration by Robert Adam.

NEO-GREC (or GREEK REVIVAL): began about 1795, extended into the opening decades of the nineteenth century, and did not actually yield to the revived gothic until the 1840s.

VICTORIAN: 1830–1900. There was a revival of the gothic, Elizabethan, Renaissance, and rococo, an eclecticism that left its imprint on ceramics, which were often florid and overly decorated.

Mark

It is common practice to pick up an object and turn it over for a look at the bottom with the expectation of finding a mark. Often there is none. Actually, the mark is the least reliable of all the factors, since in many cases it is missing and many times faked. It was not until 1724 that the Meissen factory adopted as a regular mark the crossed swords of the arms of Saxony. This mark was invariably painted in underglaze blue on the base. Other European porcelain and faience factories quickly followed the lead of Meissen, and in 1766 the porcelain makers of France were required by law to use a mark that had been previously registered with the police authorities.

The practice of marking was never regulated, however, with the result that factories proud of their work used a recognized mark, while the less important factories either left their wares unmarked or used a mark similar to a famous one. The crossed swords of Meissen were used on numerous imitations and quite openly copied on Bow, Derby, Worcester, and Lowestoft in England.

Many marks encountered on ceramics are merely those of painters or workmen and are not a guide to the place of manufacture, even when identified, for these people often worked in many different factories.

It is important to know that ceramics are marked in different ways. They were incised, impressed, printed, or painted. Incised marks are scratched into the body before the first firing process and before decoration. Signature and initial marks were often done in this form. The edges are apt to show a plowed-up effect, which does not occur with impressed marks. Impressed marks are made by applying a metal die to the ware before the first firing and decoration. This process is most commonly used with a simple name. The standard WEDGWOOD is a good example. An impressed seal-type mark made up of initials, monogram, or other devices is on much twentieth-century studio pottery. Printed marks first came into general use about 1800, though they were on porcelains decorated with underglaze-blue patterns as early as 1760. In the course of manufacture the printed pattern or mark is transferred to the article by transfer printing. This process may take place either before or after glazing. As a general rule ceramics having a printed pattern also have a printed mark. Most twentieth-century potters apply their printed marks by means of a rubber stamp or stencil. Painted marks are applied over the glaze during or after decorating. Typical examples are the red and gold anchor marks of Chelsea and the painted "Spode" mark. Some early porcelains decorated in underglaze blue have marks painted in blue underglaze. Applied marks are rare. They could be classed with impressed marks, as in most cases they are impressed marks on a raised pad. The potter formed them separately and placed them in position before firing. An example is the raised anchor mark of Chelsea. In this book, marks are rendered as they appear: either in all capital letters (WEDGWOOD, D.B.D., C.B. D.), or in upper- and lower-case letters ("Spode").

The beginning collector should approach all marks with caution. It is most important to detect the difference between the various materials. Is it earthenware, hard paste porcelain, soft paste porcelain, or bone china? After determining this, you immediately realize that an object with a neat anchor on its Chelsea-type figure cannot possibly be a product of that factory if the body is a hard Continental paste. In attempting to identify an article, approach it with an unbiased mind, holding no preconceived opinion, and then carefully consider all five factors before attempting to settle on an identification.

V

Chinese Porcelain

It is natural that when we think of porcelain our minds should turn to the country of China, the birthplace of true, or hard paste, porcelain. Porcelain has been made there for more than a thousand years; consequently the subject is enormous, well known to only a moderate number of scholars. There are several basic facts, however, that the beginner will want to know in order to add to his enjoyment and appreciation.

Chinese porcelain is known by the dynasties in which it was produced, and in the Ming and Ch'ing dynasties by the emperor as well. Following is a table of dynasties and dates in the way they are usually referred to.

T'ang Dynasty:	A.D. 608–906
Sung Dynasty:	960–1279
Yüan, or Mongol, Dynasty:	1280–1367
Ming Dynasty:	1368–1643

PERIOD:

Hung-wu	1368–1398
Chien-wen	1399–1402
Yung-lo	1403–1424
Hung-hsi	1425–1426
Hsüan-te	1426–1435
Cheng-t'ung	1436–1449
Ching-t'ai	1450–1456
T'ien-shun	1457–1464
Ch'eng-hua	1465–1487
Hung-chih	1488–1505
Cheng-te	1506–1521
Chia-ching	1522–1566
Lung-ch'ing	1567–1572
Wan-li	1573–1619
T'ai-ch'ang	1620–1621
T'ien-ch'i	1621–1643
Ch'ung-cheng	1628–1643

Ch'ing, or Manchu, Dynasty	1644–1912

PERIOD:

Shun-chih	1644–1661
K'ang-hsi	1662–1722
Yung-cheng	1723–1735
Ch'ien-lung	1736–1795
Chia-ch'ing	1796–1820
Tao-kuang	1821–1850
Hsien-feng	1851–1861
T'ung-chih	1862–1874
Kuang-hsü	1875–1908
Hsüan-t'ung	1909–1912

It is useful to know that the custom is to speak of old Chinese porcelain as belonging to the reign of Wan-li or K'ang-hsi rather than designating it merely as Ming or Ch'ing. But it is sufficient for the novice to remember the more important dynasties—Sung, Ming, and Ch'ing—with their dates, and the names K'ang-hsi and Ch'ien-lung in the Ch'ing Dynasty. During the reigns of these two emperors porcelain was elevated to a very high position and, since it was also exported to Europe in vast quantities, much of it is still available.

The first great period of Chinese ceramics was the T'ang Dynasty. The majority of the pieces that have survived are those which have been excavated from tombs, and they were not known to the European market until the twentieth century. With the introduction of Buddhism in the fifth century, the Chinese began to execute much figure sculpture, which pointed the way to the human and animal figures produced during the T'ang Dynasty. Some of these are glazed and some unglazed, but originally all were decorated with brightly colored pigments. The surviving pottery shows a developing quality of vigor and a variety of techniques and color. Owing to burial and to rough handling during excavation, many of these figures have been damaged and later restored. They were normally made of coarse, whitish pottery, slightly resembling plaster of Paris and easily susceptible to damage. They have been much copied by forgers in recent years, and the novice is not apt to find true T'ang outside a museum. However, the faker finds it hard to copy the wonderful proportions and simple lines. The T'ang wares include such widely varied styles as a soft-white-to-light-colored, lead-glazed earthenware approaching porcelain in hardness, but opaque, a brown-glazed feldspathic stoneware, and a fine white, greenish porcelain.

The Sung Dynasty is frequently referred to as the classic period of all Chinese art. In ceramics, it is famous for its celadon, white, and deep-brown glazed wares. The most important are the rare articles made especially for the emperor and his court, referred to as Kuan ware, meaning "official," or "imperial." Kuan ware is of the highest quality, and fine specimens exist in a number of collections. The dark body is often thinner than the glaze, which is opaque, vitrified, and sometimes irregularly crackled and ranges in color from a pale bluish-green through blue to dove-gray. Sung imperial ware is elegant, quiet, and restrained.

Ting ware, produced during the Sung Dynasty, was among the first true porcelains made. It is translucent orange when held against a strong light and is covered in a thin, colorless glaze, often with an ivory tinge. The pieces were normally fired upside down, and frequently the unglazed rim was protected by a thin copper band. The thin foot rims are normally glazed. Many of the pieces are plain, but occasionally they have either finely incised or molded decoration that produces an impression of flowers, birds, and fish. The figures of humans and animals so prolific during the T'ang Dynasty had almost ceased being made because it was no longer the custom to be buried with such objects, and the forms of Ting ware are the classic ones, *mei-p'ing* (a baluster vase with a narrow lip), bottles with everted lips, stem cups, saucer dishes, lobed bowls, and shallow bowls, as well as boxes, ewers, and waterpots. Again the beginning collector is unlikely to see Sung objects other than in a museum.

In 1279 the last Sung emperor was overthrown by the Mongols, and the Yüan Dynasty of Kublai Khan began. The Yüan continued the techniques of the Sung potters, and it is difficult to be sure whether an article of ceramics dates from Sung or Yüan times. The one important innovation that began during the Yüan Dynasty was decorating porcelain with cobalt (blue) and copper (red) under the glaze, colors that were brought in from the Near East. This method of painting under the glaze came from the Persians.

Ming

Porcelain produced under the Ming Dynasty is the most widely known, because it is the first Chinese period whose works are extant in large numbers, it is the last period that can be designated as truly Chinese, and it was the first porcelain to reach the Western world. Whereas the Sung Dynasty is often considered the classic period, Ming is considered the baroque, with massive forms and intricate designs. Before the Ming Dynasty, dynasty names had been based upon the surname of the dynastic founder—as with T'ang and Sung—but the founder of the Ming Dynasty, Chu Yüan-chang, a priest with an eye for publicity, designated his reign as "*ming*," or "bright." In the matter of the arts posterity agrees that his boast was fulfilled.

The activity of the Ming potters was vast. The leading pottery town was Ching-te-chen in the province of Kiangsi. It was here that the first Ming emperor, Hung-wu, rebuilt the imperial kilns in 1369. It is known that kilns were active there in the tenth century. By the middle of the fifteenth century Ching-te-chen had become the greatest ceramic center in China. It was ideally situated near Poyang Lake, whence its products could go by lake and river to Nanking and by the grand canal to Peking. An apparently inexhaustible supply of china clay lay in the Ma-ch'ang hills nearby, while across the river at Hu-t'ien was to be found the other ingredient in the manufacture of porcelain, china stone. Ching-te-chen produced porcelain in enormous quantities. In a single year, 1554, Emperor Chia-ching required

26,350 bowls with dragons in blue, 30,500 plates, 6,900 wine cups, 680 large garden fish bowls, 28,800 tea cups, 600 libation cups, 6,000 ewers, and 10,200 bowls.

Though Ching-te-chen was the largest Ming porcelain center, there were other factories that were commercial, capitalistic ventures, producing monochrome wares. A white porcelain was made at Te-hua in Fukien as early as the Sung Dynasty. The Fukien wares are in a special category. They never bear reign dates and are difficult to date accurately. They range in quality from the finest porcelain —with a luminous, warm, and lustrous glaze with a brownish tint where it runs thick—to the more metallic products of the last hundred years.

It is possible for amateurs to recognize certain Ming pieces (or imitations of the Ming manner) with reasonable accuracy. There is first of all the famous blue-and-white work, a Ming specialty. On seeing a white jar with blue dragons, blue waves, or other blue designs, you may safely guess that it is Ming, provided the color has been painted in flat washes or in carefully pencilled lines, and not, as in the later K'ang-hsi work, in graded depths. The blue was put on under the glaze, sometimes cool and grayish and sometimes dark. The characteristic tone was made possible by the importation from the Near East of the famous Mohammedan blue. The imported color was mixed with native cobalt, and the Ming potters became dependent on it, the quality of their blue failing to a great extent whenever the Mohammedan blue was not available.

Painting on porcelain in underglaze cobalt blue, making what we call "blue-and-white," has been the most widespread of all forms of ceramic decoration. Chinese blue-and-white was fired only once. The body was allowed to dry; then the pigment (color) was applied to the unglazed body, the whole covered with glaze, and the piece fired all in one session. Because of the kinship of the materials of the glaze and paste, fusion is complete. It took several days in the kiln to vitrify the clay and turn it into porcelain. Finally the kilns cooled and the articles were removed.

Cobalt appears gray on the unglazed body and turns blue during the process of firing. With the exceptions of manganese purple and copper red, cobalt was the only color that could withstand the necessary high temperature of the kiln. There was great variety in the color of the blue, depending on the purity of the cobalt and its concentration in the glaze. The Chinese did not have a native source of cobalt free from manganese, which accounts for the great importance attached to the imported Mohammedan blue. The cobalt obtained from the Persians was quite pure and brilliant in color. Methods were developed throughout the Ming Dynasty for separating the impurities from cobalt, and by the end of the Ming Dynasty, cobalt was produced that was sufficiently pure to give an excellent color.

Polychrome decoration began approximately with the reign of Chia-ching (1522–1566). By the time of Wan-li (1573–1619) the practice of painting with enamel colors on the finished fired glaze had been established.

The first direct exportation of Chinese porcelain to Europe occurred early in the sixteenth century. These early shipments consisted entirely of blue-and-white. From this time on, an increasingly large quantity of porcelain was exported to Europe, initially to Portugal and subsequently to Holland and other countries. The supply of export pieces to Europe during this period must have been immense in light of the large number of surviving relics.

Ch'ing Dynasty

The political disturbances that attended the passing of the Ming Dynasty and the establishment of the Ch'ing Manchus were unfavorable to material progress at the Ching-te-chen factory, but when order was restored and Emperor K'ang-hsi set upon the throne in 1662, the golden age of Chinese porcelain had arrived. There followed more than sixty years of artistic development in ceramics that has never been equalled or excelled. The K'ang-hsi blue-and-white reached a technical excellence never surpassed. The porcelain, pure white and of fine texture, is covered with a glaze of slightly bluish or greenish tint, and the decoration, at its best, is in a pure blue of great luminosity. Potters the world over have attempted from time to time to imitate this ware without success. To be K'ang-hsi blue-and-white, a piece must possess the following five points:

1. The blue must be true in color tone.
2. The white must be the purest.
3. The drawing must be fine and clear in shading and outline.
4. The shape must be of irreproachable elegance.
5. The glaze must be very brilliant and undamaged.

K'ang-hsi blue-and-white was made from 1683 onward and aroused much interest in Europe in the eighteenth and nineteenth centuries. A single piece could pass through as many as seventy hands for various forms of decoration before it was ready for firing.

The period is also famous for large vases whose monumental grandeur of form, with emphasis on height, was matched by strong painted decoration. Much of this painting was done in easily fusible enamel colors, applied over the glaze after the vessel had received its preliminary firing. These colors are grouped and known variously as *famille noire* (black), *famille verte* (brilliant copper green, manganese purple, antimony yellow, overglaze blue, and iron red), *famille rose* (a rose-pink introduced from Europe), and the rare *famille jaune* (yellow).

In 1699 K'ang-hsi opened the Port of Canton to a restricted but legally sanctioned foreign trade. European countries were allowed to conduct business and build their own warehouses, called "hongs," on the docks. Purchases of tea, silks, and porcelain could be made on the ships contiguous to the docks, but foreigners were not permitted to travel through China or to learn the language. The Chinese looked upon the Europeans as barbarians. Chinese middlemen, called "hong merchants," were appointed to fill the orders for the European trade.

Ch'ien-lung blue-and-white is supposed to be inferior to K'ang-hsi. This is true of some of the export wares, but there are instances where the drawing is fine and the color good. Many high-quality pieces of blue-and-white dating from the reigns of Yung-cheng and Ch'ien-lung copy fifteenth-century originals, sometimes bearing the correct marks and sometimes the marks of the pieces they resemble. It is usually fairly easy to distinguish the eighteenth-century copies, since black spotting has been added deliberately instead of appearing accidentally as it did on the originals. The paste has a somewhat more marked orange-peel texture, and the drawing is not so free. Much Yung-cheng and Ch'ien-lung enamelled porcelain is painted in a detailed and somewhat stereotyped miniature style, which may be contrasted with the usually freer manner practiced under K'ang-hsi.

During the reign of K'ang-hsi very few pieces bear a mark, because Ch'ang Ch'i, the superintendent of the imperial factories between 1677 and 1680, issued an edict forbidding the potters to use the reign mark of the emperor on their wares. It is impossible to tell how effective this order was, but the number of pieces either without a mark or with merely an artemisia leaf, a lotus blossom, an endless knot, an incense burner, or another symbol within a double circle suggests that it was obeyed.

Identification

The body, or paste, of Chinese porcelain is not of uniform quality. The Chinese attached no particular value to the quality of translucence. In their estimation, resonance was of greater importance in judging the physical merits of a piece. In much of the purest Chinese porcelain the walls are thick and the paste translucent only at the thinnest parts. The body color of a good amount of old Chinese porcelain with blue decoration, or of that in which blue predominates, has a slightly bluish tinge much like the color of very poor skimmed milk.

Articles commonly made of porcelain included vessels for temple or sacrificial use and for domestic shrines, all kinds of writing paraphernalia, every kind of vase, jar, or bowl for flowers (the Chinese, being a flower-loving people, required a large supply of such items), wine cups, trays, teapots, tea caddies, tea cups or bowls (as porcelain has an insulating quality, the Chinese placed no handles on their cups or tea bowls), plates, platters, bottles, drum or barrel-shaped garden seats, lanterns, fish bowls, covered jars for sweetmeats or ginger, plaques for the embellishment of furniture, figures or statuettes, and a host of minor odds and ends. In addition to these, there were table services and other miscellaneous articles made for general export to Europe and America, which are further detailed in the following chapter.

A wide variety of subjects appear in the decoration of Chinese porcelain. To name a few, there are symbolic and emblematic charms, characters, lozenges, coins, rhinoceros' horns, bamboo, storks, tortoises, fir trees, bats, and Buddhistic lions, erroneously called "kylins." Each has a particular meaning, and often their combination tells a story. The English, in imitating the Chinese porcelain, made no effort to learn the significance of these objects, using them indiscriminately. As a result the English copies make no allegorical sense.

The subject of Chinese porcelain is more interesting when one is aware that the bird that resembles a peacock or pheasant (*feng-huang*) is supposed to live in the highest heavens and is a symbol for beauty and perfection, that the hare (*t'u*) is seen in the moon, where it is preparing the elixir of life, that the "kylin" is a strange animal that represents happiness and perfection also. The dragon (*lung*) appears in many forms—as the symbol of spring, the emblem of the emperor, and also a herald of storms and rain. Five claws indicate the rank of emperor and also princes of the first and second rank. The deer (*lu*) represents long life, and the bat (*fu*) stands for happiness and good fortune. These are just a few of the symbols.

Marks

The marks on Chinese porcelain occur in three classes: date marks, hall and other allied marks, and symbol marks. Marks are usually found on the base of a piece and most commonly are painted in blue. On some of the later pieces they are in red. They may also be engraved in the paste or stand out in relief.

The marks that are found may not be dependable—indeed, many pieces are not marked at all and others have marks that are forged and misapplied. Falsifying marks is a practice that has gone on for centuries. The mark on a piece of Chinese porcelain may tell the truth, but more likely it tells a falsehood. Under these circumstances, it is safer for the novice to disregard the mark and to judge the piece by its visible and tangible qualities.

VI

Chinese Export
or Lowestoft?

Confusion continues as to what so-called Lowestoft china
really is. Is this a misnomer? If so, then what should it be
called? Lowestoft is a false attribution; Chinese Export
porcelain is correct. It is also referred to as Chinese or
Oriental Lowestoft, China Trade porcelain, and India Company china. The latter name is widely used on the Continent and derived from the fact that originally almost all
porcelain of this type was brought from China in the ships
of the East India trading companies of Holland, England,
Denmark, Sweden, France, Portugal, and Austria.

The confusion in labelling arose when William Chaffers,

an outstanding English authority on ceramics, in the first edition of his book *Marks and Monograms on European and Oriental Pottery and Porcelain*, published in 1876, erroneously credited all porcelain of this type to a small factory located at Lowestoft, England. In spite of the fact that this error was corrected in later editions, the damage was done, with the result that the name has persisted to this day, to the confusion of many novice collectors. (There *was* a small porcelain factory located at Lowestoft, England, fully discussed in Chapter XII, which produced a soft paste china far different from the hard paste, or true, porcelain of Chinese Export.)

Export ware was also made at the Ching-te-chen factories and was decorated either there or by artists at enamel works outside the city of Canton. The products were transported overland and by river and lakes from Ching-te-chen to Canton, where they were loaded aboard the ships of various East India companies and, after 1784, on American ships for transport to the United States. Western ships sailed from their home ports around the Cape of Good Hope, across the Indian Ocean, and finally up the China coast to the Portuguese colony of Macao. Here they awaited a pilot who would guide them up river to Canton, where the trade center was established. Orders for porcelain were received in Canton by the Chinese hong merchants. Since it normally required the shipments of china seven months to make the journey from Ching-te-chen to Canton, it became customary for the hong merchants to maintain a supply of stock designs in their Canton shops. When specific orders called for the addition of initials, crests, or a decorative device, Cantonese enamellers applied such details over the glaze.

The majority of this porcelain was imported by the European countries from the early 1700s to 1800. It was imported into the United States directly from China from

1784, when the *Empress of China* sailed from New York, until around 1845, when the market for porcelain was largely taken over by the English manufacturers.

The Chinese were eager to produce the porcelain in the forms most acceptable to the various foreign buyers. These forms were alien to their own Chinese customs and usage and did not appeal to the native market. The form and the style of decoration are the major differences between Chinese Export and Chinese porcelain made for home consumption. Since the china was made to order for the European and American buyers, it is safe to assume that any forms and shapes used in eighteenth-century Europe were likely to turn up in Chinese Export. Among these are mugs, tea cups and tea bowls, tea caddies, trays, teapots, coffeepots, creamers, candlesticks, two-, three-, and five-piece garnitures, and pistol handle urns made for the European and American taste. Whether your interest is family history, maritime affairs, sport, horticulture, mythology, or national glory, Chinese porcelain made for export provides endless examples.

The surface of the glaze on this true, or hard paste, porcelain varied widely, from the almost white, smooth, fine quality eggshell tea bowls and saucers made in the middle of the eighteenth century to the uneven surface described as orange peel found on some of the heavier pieces toward the end of the eighteenth and in the early nineteenth centuries. Chinese Export has a translucent bluish, greenish, or grayish cast. Sometimes this background cast varies in color, according to its position in the kiln. One characteristic imperfection of the surface is the tiny dark specks that vary in size from pin points to several times that size.

Chinese Export, unlike some Chinese porcelain made for home consumption, *never has any factory or other marks on the back.* (There is one armorial service made for the Chadwick family that has on the back "Canton in China, January, 1791," but this and one or two similar inscriptions are in the nature of customs inscriptions rather than a manufacturer's mark.) Another point to note is that all bottom surfaces upon which the pieces rest *are never glazed*. These include the bottoms of platters, dishes, cups, and vases, teapot rims, the rims of all covers, and the inside area upon which the covers rested.

Chinese Export porcelain falls into three main categories:

Chinese Export for the European market	1700–1800
Blue-and-white export wares made for all markets	1700–1830
Chinese Export made for the American market	1785–1845

Because the ship's captain, when he placed his order with the hong merchants, often brought with him a piece of china or a drawing of a crest or design to be copied on the dinner set or ornaments he was commissioning the hong merchant to supply, the china exported to the different countries shows characteristics of design indigenous to that particular country. With a little study, you can tell which European market commissioned an article of Chinese Export.

Porcelains decorated in underglaze blue depicting landscapes and river scenes were made during the K'ang-hsi period (1662–1722) and the Yung-cheng, Ch'ien-lung, and Chia-ch'ing periods (1723–1820). From these evolved a group of wares known as "Nanking," or "Nankeen." Nanking was first produced in the 1780s at Ching-te-chen and was sent from there to Canton via the northern water route and the city of Nanking.

At first these porcelains were of a very fine quality. Their designs were of flowers, landscapes, or river scenes used in combination with several different borders. When these various central scenes are combined with a latticework band surrounding a post-and-spear design, the piece is Nanking. Overglaze gilt highlights are occasionally found on this china, and, contrary to general opinion, they were added by Chinese artists more often than by Europeans.

Because the trade demanded great quantities of cheap wares, similar underglaze-blue river scenes, which came to be known as "Canton," were also produced. The central landscape-with-river theme had the same elements as Nanking, but the border was different: cross-hatching edged with an inner scalloped outline. Only the Canton pattern has this scalloped border.

The familiar Willow pattern used so extensively in transfer design by English potters was derived from these two patterns—not an exact copy by any means but the English potters' interpretation of the Chinese painting.

Probably the most interesting of the late-eighteenth-century Chinese export patterns is that known as "Fitzhugh." The original Fitzhugh pattern consisted of a central medallion surrounded by four stylized floral panels representing the Chinese arts. Its border was an exuberant yet stylized combination of trellis, diapering, butterflies, traditional Chinese fruits and flowers, and a Chinese fret grouped in a tight series of repeats. Often the central medallion was replaced by symbols or initials. In addition to being produced in underglaze blue, Fitzhugh was also made in orange, brown, mulberry pink, black, green, and yellow.

Rose Medallion, Mandarin, and Rose Canton were popular nineteenth-century patterns enamelled in a polychrome palette. Rose Medallion has a placement of pattern similar to Fitzhugh, consisting of a gilded medallion surrounded by panels of floral groups alternating with mandarin scenes. These panels are surrounded by rose-pink peonies and green foliage on a gilt or white background. Sometimes other designs, such as black butterflies, are added. The entire design is painted in very thick enamels, the quality of paint-

Chinese Export underglaze-blue reticulated fruit bowl.
Canton, showing cloud border, c. 1825.

Chinese Export underglaze-blue salad bowl.
Nanking, with post and spear border, c. 1825.

Chinese Export plate in underglaze blue.
Fitzhugh medallion and floral panels. Nanking border, c. 1825.

ing varying to a great extent. This pattern has never lost favor and is still being produced today. (See color insert, Chinese Export "Rose Medallion" plate.)

Composition and decorative detail on Mandarin ware were also inspired by the Fitzhugh pattern, and Mandarin-decorated porcelains are often confused with Rose Medallion. They usually have a single scene or several panel scenes of Chinese figures. The border decoration on the more typical pieces is of flowers, butterflies, and birds on a gold ground. The elements that make up this pattern, as well as Rose Medallion and Rose Canton, are derived from the patterns made for the native Chinese market in the seventeenth and early eighteenth centuries known as *famille rose* and *famille verte* and from the early *famille rose*–decorated porcelain made for the European export trade. Variations on the Mandarin porcelains made for export are endless. In the earlier pieces the figures have little or no background around or behind them and they are often identified wrongly as Rose Medallion.

Rose Canton is also often confused with Rose Medallion, because its enamel colors are identical and rose-colored peonies are prevalent and the general effect is thus quite similar. Some authorities classify all these patterns as Rose Canton, since they have the same essential features.

The dating of Rose Medallion and Rose Canton is in question. It was first thought that these patterns were not made or exported before the 1800s. However, the presence of features from these designs on pieces known to be earlier because of their shape and other decoration has changed the dating considerably. Familiarity with only the late and poorly done pieces has led to a general disregard for this porcelain as good Export, although earlier pieces of fine workmanship and coloring can be of exceptional beauty. Unfortunately, the majority of the Rose Medallion that is seen on the market today is the late and inferior type.

In the past few years, with its increased popularity, there has been an explosion in the price of Chinese Export in spite of the fact that enormous amounts of it were exported to Europe and America. This ware, which we prize so dearly today, was shipped as ballast in the sailing vessels of the time. The earlier pieces and those in proof condition naturally bring the highest prices, but even repaired articles of an unusual nature command a good price.

Anyone who contemplates the collection of Chinese Export should be aware of the existence of the nineteenth-century Samson copies. These were produced by Samson & Company of 7 rue Béranger, Paris, manufacturers from 1845 onward of "Reproductions of Ancient works emanating from the Museums and from private collections." The claim was made that all such reproductions were distinctly marked. On the copies of Chinese Export a seal with pseudo-Chinese marks was applied. Beware if this mark is found, or any evidence that one has been removed. Many pieces may have been unmarked. Samson china is a good-quality hard paste porcelain, but it is not Chinese Export and consequently commands a far lower price than that enjoyed by the genuine article.

VII

Delft, or
Tin-Glazed Earthenware

European concern and interest over the blue-and-white porcelain being imported from China by the Dutch East India merchants resulted in an effort to produce a similar ware. Tin-glazed earthenware was a first attempt by Holland and England to copy Chinese blue-and-white. It was admittedly an imitation of the *appearance* and not an imitation of the qualities peculiar to porcelain.

The method of painting white enamel on brown earthenware originated from the potter's natural desire to procure a surface upon which his color decorations would show up well. In time, a process developed whereby a soft earthenware of natural color was covered by a thick coating of

Dutch delft plate decorated for the English market, c. 1760.
The brownish clay pottery of the body
and opaque white glaze show clearly where it is chipped.

white, opaque enamel. The glaze was made opaque with ashes of oxide of tin. The decorator painted his pattern or picture swiftly and irrevocably on the white absorbent surface as though he were working in water color. In Holland, where there were refinements of the process, the design was often covered with a second transparent lead glaze to give richness and depth, and the whole was fired together at a high temperature. At times, other and more sensitive colors were added and the pieces fired again at a lower temperature in a muffle kiln.

The earliest use of tin-oxide glaze goes back to about 1000 B.C., when Babylonian brick reliefs were decorated with it, although nothing else of the kind is seen between 500 B.C. and the eighth century, when this glaze was rediscovered by Persian potters. Moslem conquests spread the knowledge along the northern coast of Africa into Moorish Spain, whence it passed to Italy by way of the island of Maiolica (now Majorca), and to Faience, in France, where it did not gain a foothold until later. In the late sixteenth century, an industry using this method grew up in the city of Delft in Holland, and soon crossed the Channel to England. Tin-glazed ware is classified according to its place of origin for each country: in Italy it is called "majolica," in France and other European countries "faience," and in Holland and England "delftware."

Delft was first produced in Holland about the year 1602. In the early seventeenth century, Dutch potters made only ceramics painted in blue, crowded with figures and ornaments in the Chinese style. Dutch potters are rightly renowned for their painting, but they seem to have lacked imagination and, when not imitating Far Eastern shapes, fell to crude modelling of bizarre, eccentric, and unlikely objects.

Tiles, an important product of the Delft tin-glaze factories, were painted with figure subjects, ships, landscapes,

*"Boy-in-Swing," French faience plate depicting
a naïve provincial subject, c. 1770.*

and flowers in blue early in the seventeenth century, but later in manganese purple and even in polychrome. Table objects and drug and tobacco jars were produced in delft as well.

Dutch delft was imported into England and was in general use by the seventeenth century. The close connection of the royal house of England with Holland accelerated the fashion of displaying delft in cabinets. William of Orange brought large amounts of blue-and-white delft to Hampton Court, and it soon appeared everywhere.

Delft was made in England by Flemish and Dutch refugees for many years before it was produced by English potters. Lambeth must be credited with the best results in English delft. However, it had been made earlier in other London areas, particularly Southwark. By 1665 there were about twenty potters working there. Manufacture must have increased rapidly, since by 1672 a royal proclamation forbade the importation of "painted earthenware" to compete with the same production "but lately found out in England." Other centers of English delft were Liverpool, from 1710 to *c.* 1780, where many punch bowls with ship decorations were made; Bristol, from the latter part of the seventeenth century to 1770; and Wincanton, Somerset, from about 1730.

The word "delftware" is often used on modern imitations, usually gift china; for example, Dutch figures in "national" costume. These pieces are made of hard-fired earthenware covered with a slip and painted under a lead glaze. It is nothing like the work done on the porous tin glaze, and the inscription "delftware" is a guarantee that it is nothing of the kind.

It is comparatively easy to identify old delft. It has a porous body (Dutch delft being more porous than the tin-glazed wares made by the English), and the brown body is covered by a thick coating of white enamel (other earthenware when glazed was covered with a translucent coating). The colors, of course, are overglaze.

Forgeries

Dutch delft, or tin-glazed earthenware, has been widely reproduced in Holland, Paris, and northern France. Samson copies are particularly good and, like those of northern France, a fairly risky purchase, since they are not easy to detect. On the copies made in northern France, there is often a crazing of the glaze that is rarely seen in genuine examples, and they are apt to be heavier.

There were factories in Holland that were established to make nothing else but good copies of delft. Although these can be regarded as a continuation of traditional styles, they should not cost as much as the rare eighteenth-century articles.

VIII

Meissen, Commonly Called Dresden

After Johann Friedrich Böttger found through his experiments that kaolin was the necessary ingredient for producing a true, or hard paste, ware, Augustus II, King of Poland and Elector of Saxony, established the great factory at Meissen, on the Elbe, about twelve miles from Dresden, and Böttger was appointed director. This was by far the most important eighteenth-century porcelain factory in Europe. Its products are commonly but erroneously called Dresden, and people find it difficult to abandon "Dresden," a household word, for the more accurate "Meissen."

Böttger died in 1719, and, with the advent of J. G. Höroldt, a new era began, often termed "the painters' period," which lasted from 1720 to about 1735. Under Höroldt, or Herold, the factory developed considerably. During this period painting of a superior character, improved gilding, and beautiful ground colors—maroon, apple green, canary yellow, and pale mauve—were introduced. They appear on the vases and table services produced at this time. On the table services the ground colors are found on the undersides of the saucers, a method of decoration copied from the Chinese.

1731 saw the added service of an eminent sculptor, Johann Kändler. The most prized Meissen are the modelled groups, figures, vases, and animals attributed to him. His famous crinoline groups, the harlequin figures, and the bold lifelike models of animals and birds are exceedingly valuable.

About 1740 the more rococo designs affected by French fashions became popular. The arcadian shepherds and shepherdesses, courtiers, musicians, peasants, mendicants, peddlers, and cupids in fancy costumes produced are elegant and dainty, although lacking the vigor and strength of Kändler's art. The tableware was flowery and picturesque, but somewhat frivolous and effeminate. It is generally held that the cream of Meissen occurred between about 1730 and 1760.

The greatest prosperity of the factories followed the Seven Years' War, from around 1763 to 1774. The King took a personal interest in the directorship of the works during this time, hence it is called the "King's Period," or "Saxe au Point," by collectors, and it is identified by a dot between the hilts of the usual crossed swords of the underglaze-blue mark.

An alteration of style in forms and models was introduced when François Acier, a noted sculptor from Paris, was employed. He designed in the French manner prevalent at Sèvres. There was considerable friction between Acier and Kändler, which was solved by allowing each to select half the designs for new models. Kändler died in 1775 and Acier retired in 1781. During this period the rococo of Louis XV changed to the classic lines of Louis XVI.

Count Camillo Marcolini was appointed director in 1774, beginning a cycle, continuing until 1820, marked by careful, painstaking work, although it lacked the freshness and vigor of the Kändler period and the charm and delicacy of the Acier. A favorite decoration was a carefully painted subject still in the rococo Watteau style, but also in the classical manner of Angelica Kauffmann, all in a rich royal blue. Figures with lacework decorations were produced in considerable quantities. A clever effect was rendered by placing real net that had been dipped in a solution of china clay on the figure. Fired in the kiln, the lace net was destroyed, leaving a "negative" of china lace. How this effect was produced often puzzles amateurs. (A "typical Meissen figure of the period is illustrated in the color insert.)

The shadow pictures called "lithophanes" came into fashion about 1828. It was one of many techniques and styles that the Meissen works tried out with the object of capturing new or enlarging markets. Lithophanes were usually flat plaques of fine-quality biscuit porcelain with molded intaglio decoration intended to be viewed only by transmitted light. By ordinary light it is extremely difficult to see what the subject is supposed to be. They resemble porcelain with an irregular surface on one side.

Under Heinrich Gottlob Kühn, director from 1833 to 1870, commercial prosperity was once more achieved. The rococo was revived, and hundreds of "Dresden" figures were made—child musicians playing instruments, dessert baskets on lofty pedestals, candelabra, and mythological groups for table centerpieces. The colors they were decorated in give the late date away. After 1870 an attempt was made to produce articles in the contemporary style, and figures of soldiers in spiked helmets with fierce mustaches, sports-

Meissen hard paste porcelain platter, c. 1820, showing the careful, painstaking work of the preceding Marcolini Period. The "crossed sword" marks are generally reliable.

women in the dress of the times, and bathing belles were
made that, if not artistically significant, are social docu-
ments. The renaissance of Meissen belongs to the twentieth
century.

Collecting porcelains of the eighteenth century is difficult,
for little has been available for some time. During 250 years
quantities have been broken, and two world wars have
brought great destruction to Meissen, both that in private
and public collections. These wars, however, also brought
some good Meissen porcelain onto the market. Economic
conditions forced many a collector to dispose of his treasures, and public institutions sold pieces from their collections to raise needed funds, but novice collectors should
keep in mind that sellers sometimes falsely claim articles to
be eighteenth-century and from a fine collection when in
truth they have been made in the past few years and are
of far less value. Remember that the Meissen factory is
still in operation in East Germany. It is very disappointing
to have to tell servicemen and tourists who have bought
such articles that they are worth much less than they paid
for them.

Marks and Frauds

It is probable that most beginners are familiar with the
usual Meissen mark—crossed swords—taken from the
Electoral arms of Saxony. There were some additional
marks, and the underglaze-blue crossed swords changed
from time to time.

The earliest mark on Meissen porcelain was the cipher
A.R. for Augustus Rex, King Augustus II, "The Strong"
(reigning from 1697 to 1704 and 1709 to 1733), and Augustus III (1733–1763). This mark occurred on pieces originally intended for the royal palaces or as royal gifts (not

always used as intended). It is much more common on the porcelain of the 1725–1730 period than later.

 The earlier forms of the crossed swords tended to be carefully drawn, with pommels and curved guards.

 A dot between the hilts of the crossed swords was used during the "King's Period"—1763 to 1774.

 A star between the hilts was used from 1774 to 1814, the "Marcolini Period."

On white porcelain vessels without defects, a nick in the paste was made across the swords. This mark indicated that the piece was sold "in the white" out of the factory and that the painting and gilding was done by *Hausmaler*, men and women, often excellent decorators, who obtained white wares from the factory and painted them at home.

 In the mark for defective porcelain the number of lines is supposed to indicate good, medium, and outcast.

A dot between the points of the sword, not to be confused with the dot between the hilts, is on porcelain dating from 1924 and later.

Of the imitators' marks, the one most ridiculously forged was the very early Meissen cipher A.R., which was used between 1725 and 1730. The china that until fairly recently bore this fraudulent mark was not made at the state factory of Meissen but by a private firm named Wolfsohn in the town of Dresden, owned by Madam Helena Wolfsohn. It was produced from about 1850 to about 1880, when Madam Wolfsohn was prevented by injunction from further use of the mark.

Other imitators' marks are the crossed swords with an M for Meyer and Son, a late-nineteenth-century Dresden factory; crossed swords with a T between the swords, the factory of Hamann and Thieme, founded in 1875; and crossed swords with an S, from the factory of Edmé Samson & Company of Paris, after 1845. When the word "Dresden" is on the base of an article, it is not Meissen but a late nineteenth- or twentieth-century example of porcelain made in Dresden.

IX

German and Austrian
Porcelain Factories

Berlin Porcelain Factory (1752 to present)

The first Berlin porcelain factory was founded in 1752 by Wilhelm Kaspar Wegely with the help of runaway workmen from Höchst and was forced to close in 1757. Consequently, Wegely's porcelain is very scarce. Most surviving examples are figures in white.

Other factories succeeded Wegely's, continuing to the present day. The current one is known as the Berlin State Porcelain Manufactory. The paste produced is very hard, dense of texture, and a cold white in color. The glaze is hard, clear, brilliant, and technically perfect. Besides dinner, tea, coffee, chocolate, and breakfast sets, ornate vases and other decorative accessories were made, first in the French and rococo style, followed by the neoclassic, and in due time the Empire manner.

The mark during the early period (1752–1757) was a W, for Wegely, in underglaze blue, with the strokes of the letter crossed. Later a crudely formed G was used. When the factory became a royal possession, the mark was a scepter.

Höchst Porcelain Factory (1746–1796)

The Höchst factory succeeded in making a hard paste porcelain by 1746. The earliest wares are very primitive in appearance. They are grayish in color and have poor translucence. Improvements were made by 1753, and about this time rococo scrollwork appears on the bases of the figures. A great deal of tableware was made, and a crimson monochrome is characteristic of much of the enamel painting. Because of political conditions, the factory was closed in 1796. In addition to tableware and the usual items for decorative use, Höchst is famous for its fine figures, groups, and portrait medallions, both glazed and in the biscuit. It is sought after by collectors and brings high prices.

The usual mark is a wheel with six spokes in red or other colored enamels. Attention should be drawn to the fact that the old Höchst molds passed to other factories and were used for porcelain copies by the firms of Dressel, Kister & Company at Passau from 1840 and F. A. Mehlem of Bonn from 1836, and for faience copies by the factory at Damme from

Pair of Höchst chinoiserie *actor figures*
in white hard paste porcelain, c. 1760.

1827. The six-spoke wheel mark was used by all of them, at Damme in conjunction with the letter D.

Nymphenburg Porcelain (1747–1862)

(from 1862 to present in private hands)

The factory began in 1747 at Naudeck, but in 1761 was transferred to quarters adjacent to the palace of Nymphenburg, near Munich. The body is a paste of excellent quality, white, hard, and of dense, smooth texture. The glaze is of admirable quality, perfectly distributed, clear and brilliant. The articles made include all the customary "useful" tableware and the usual adjuncts, but the reputation of the factory rests on its fine figures and groups, which are of the greatest excellence. In shape the Nymphenburg china followed closely the fashions at Meissen. Decoration on Nymphenburg is marked by naturalism and delicacy of painting.

The reputation of the factory rests on its fine figures. The earliest were by Josef Ponnhauser, a modeller from Vienna who worked between 1754 and 1755. Bustelli, who was employed as modeller in 1754, had a superb grasp of the principles of design and produced portraits and figures from the Italian comedy. Melchior (1796–1822) modelled in the classical style of the early years of the nineteenth century. The usual mark found on Nymphenburg was some form of the Bavarian coat of arms.

Vienna China (1719–1864)

The hard paste porcelain factory at Vienna was established by 1719. From the beginning it produced work of admir-

*Nymphenburg porcelain group showing the excellent quality
of the paste, which is white, hard,
and of a dense smooth texture, c. 1755.*

able quality but was beset by financial difficulties, and in 1744 it was bought with all its recipes by Empress Maria Theresa and thereafter conducted as a royal enterprise.

From the start the glaze was good, and soon was parallel in quality with the Meissen glaze. Besides table services and decorative objects the factory produced a great quantity of very elaborate vases and other ornaments, and a large number of figures, groups, and statuettes, glazed and in the biscuit. Meissen models provided most of the shapes. Modelling in high relief, molded ornaments in low relief impressed in the paste, piercing, fretwork, painting, and gilding were freely employed in the decorative process.

The subjects of the painted decoration included polychrome Chinese motifs; Japanese birds and flowers; Imari red, blue, and gold patterns; figures and landscapes; polychrome leafy scrolls with flowers, fruits, canopies, and figures; landscapes or scenes in cartouche; and various other patterns. In addition to the lavish painted decorations, there is the enrichment of raised gilding, which required several coats, each successive coat being fired and burnished. Further ornament was engraved on this gilding.

While some of the porcelain produced in the eighteenth century at the Vienna factory was admirable, most of it was ostentatious and lacking in freshness and vigor. During the early period the majority was unmarked. After 1744, when the factory became Crown property, the Austrian shield was painted in underglaze blue with a wood block. From 1784 onward, the pieces were dated by the last two figures of the year impressed in the paste.

X

Sèvres Porcelain

It was at Vincennes, southeast of Paris, that the great royal porcelain factory of Sèvres got its start in 1738. Only experimental work was done there until 1745, when the production of a fine soft paste ware began. A company was formed in the name of Charles Adam, and Louis XV granted the first privilege giving Vincennes the sole right to make porcelain and to decorate it with figures and gilding and forbidding the workmen to go elsewhere. Duplessis, a goldsmith, directed the models, and Hellot, a chemist, superintended the selection of materials.

Production in 1745 consisted largely of the manufacture of artificial flowers in porcelain. These were given gilded bronze mounts and used on clocks, sconces, inkstands, and girondoles and in relief on vases. By 1749 they had become fashionable enough to cause a scandal and did so when the Marquis d'Argenson revealed the King's large expenditure on them.

Madame de Pompadour took a great interest in the factory. She was so entranced by these flowers that she ordered, at the expense of $32,000, a bower of them for her garden in Bellevue. They were even scented. Partially due to her influence, it was proposed in 1753 to transfer the factory to Sèvres, close to the chateau of Bellevue. The new buildings were occupied in 1756.

Financial difficulties beset Sèvres from the outset. Since they could buy Meissen and Oriental porcelain for much less, most people found the ware too expensive. In November 1759, in order to save the situation, the King undertook the whole monetary responsibility of the works. An edict was issued ordering that the factory be administered for His Majesty, and Sèvres became Crown property.

The King immediately placed restrictions on all rival ceramic factories, forbidding them to use gilding or any color other than blue on porcelain and even faience, or to make glazed or biscuit statuettes or ornaments. These restrictions explain why Chantilly and Mennecy were decorated only in blue during that period. The royal factory of Sèvres always dominated French porcelain.

In spite of these measures, Sèvres still suffered financial troubles, and the King was obliged to pay the deficits from his privy purse. Nevertheless the factory continued to put all its efforts into magnificent productions, until the royal purse was depleted and Louis XV had to send all his silver to the mint. Finally Sèvres began to make wares for popular consumption and also began to prosper. About 1769 the secret of making hard paste porcelain was purchased, and the necessary kaolin was found and quarried near Limoges. From this time to about 1804 Sèvres made both hard and soft paste porcelain.

Royal interest in the factory continued when Louis XVI became king. Marie Antoinette in particular loved the porcelain and often visited the works. On one visit she remarked that the porcelain flowers were in all colors except blue, her favorite color. To please the Queen, one of the directors chose the cornflower as a decoration, and it became very popular, not only at Sèvres but at all the porcelain factories.

During the Revolution the factory and the workers suffered, but in 1800 Napoleon appointed a mining engineer, Alexandre Brogniart, technical director. He abandoned the making of soft paste as uneconomical, improved techniques, and established the famous museum at Sèvres. Under Brogniart the productions improved technically, and many new colors were introduced. Styles followed prevailing tastes. After 1851 decline set in, but in 1876 new buildings were occupied, and a fresh spirit prevailed. Celadons, *flambés*, and the *famille rose* of Chinese porcelains were emulated.

Sèvres was first called the "Royal Porcelain of France," then in 1770 "Porcelain of the King," and later "Sèvres Porcelain." The denomination *Vieux Sèvres* (Old Sèvres) refers to all soft paste porcelain made at the Royal Manufactory from the day of its foundation up to the French Revolution.

The early, luxurious period of Sèvres soft paste porcelain lasted from 1756 to 1769. After the factory was removed from Vincennes to Sèvres, the chemical staff of Sèvres, who experimented constantly, improved the soft paste until it was brought to absolute perfection—pure, milky white, hard, and translucent. Full advantage was taken of the capacity of soft paste to take a wide range of rich colors—

turquoise, deep royal blue, the extraordinary rose Pompadour, soft and deep at the same time, that was created in honor of the King's favorite. Rarer but not less highly esteemed and sophisticated were daffodil yellow, carmine, agate gray, rust red, and grass green. A design known as *oeil de perdrix* (partridge eye) was often used on plain backgrounds. The early management of Sèvres, inspired by the extravagant notions of the court, produced splendid cabinet pieces beyond the financial reach of most buyers. Most were intended for the King's service for the furnishing of the royal palaces of Versailles, the Trianon, Marly, Bellevue, Meudon, Saint-Germain, and Fontainebleau. When this practice proved devastating, the factory began to make wares for popular consumption. Apart from the showpieces—modelled flowers, splendid vases, and ornaments—the wares made at Sèvres include dinner services of both simple and elaborate design, trays, sugar bowls, inkstands, jardinieres, tea, coffee, and chocolate services, milk jugs, table garnitures, sconces, candlesticks, basins, ewers, tobacco and snuff boxes, patch boxes, covered jars, watchcases, buttons, cane heads, thimbles, perfume and pomatum pots, needle cases, bowls, potpourri jars, gravy boats and sauce boats, many different style vases, fruit baskets, dessert services, clock cases, cups and saucers, small flower jars, and jewel caskets.

Furniture in fully developed Louis XVI style was decorated with plaques or panels of Sèvres porcelain, a feature that distinguishes it from other French styles. Madame du Barry had a large amount of it at the Pavillon de Louveciennes, which was completed and fully furnished by 1771, the date that probably marks the height of this fashion.

At first the shapes followed the contemporary rococo design of subtle shapings and curves. But even before Louis XVI became king a strong tendency toward the greater purity and simple line of the classic period came into favor. The ablest artists of the time were always employed, and the modellers and sculptors were equally distinguished. Among them were Duplessis, Clodian, and Falconet.

Aside from the ground colors used with reserved panels for elaborate painted decorations, rims, bands, or other parts were sometimes filled with diapers of lattice or trellis-work, or bright-blue or sea-green dots in conjunction with minute gold dots on the white ground. There were also paintings of landscapes or country scenes in various colors on a white ground.

Tableware was decorated with flowers scattered or in bouquets, garlands, festoons, and wreaths. Armorial designs, monograms, and ciphers were often used. The gilding was always excellent. "Jewelled Sèvres," with transparent raised enamels laid on gold, was produced by Sèvres by the beginning of the 1780s, apparently the work of the porcelain maker and the jeweller. There are many counterfeit examples of Jewelled Sèvres on the market today.

The Sèvres mark was the royal cipher, the two L's interlaced and facing each other. The date letter or letters stood between the two L's and afford an accurate means of dating the pieces, although they were not used until 1753, when on November 19 the King decreed their use. In the Sèvres museum there is a specimen with the interlaced L's enclosing the letter A and under it, in Arabic numerals, the date 1753. The works were at Vincennes until 1756; therefore the letters A, B, and C denote pieces made at Vincennes, with D commencing the Sèvres porcelain. Pieces marked with double interlaced L's and no number are considered to be made at Vincennes prior to 1753. This is not always correct, since there were some subsequent pieces also undated. Double letters with the interlaced L's were used from 1778 and ended in 1795 with R.R.

MN^{le}
Sèvres

M.I_{mp}^{le}
de Sèvres.

The first Republican Epoch (1792–1804) had the République Française mark accompanied by the word "Sèvres." In addition to this, there were various marks and monograms of painters, decorators, and gilders of the Royal Manufactory.

There are numerous forgeries of Sèvres. In fact, there are far more forgeries existing than genuine specimens. Consequently, porcelain said to be "Old Sèvres" requires very careful examination.

Of the reproductions, the factory revived its own soft paste porcelain in 1887 at a time when *Vieux Sèvres* was commanding very high prices. It was usually decorated with a turquoise ground imitation of the old *bleu céleste* and flowery Watteau-esque figures in panels. The drawing has the characteristic sentimental approach of the nineteenth century, and transfer designs, which can be easily detected with use of a magnifying glass, were often used. The gilding is much poorer than in eighteenth-century work.

The English factories Coalport and Minton made copies in the latter part of the nineteenth century. They were fairly close, and in some cases where factory marks would identify them, they have been removed. Coalport used the *bleu de roi*, the rich and prized enamel blue that in the eighteenth century was peculiar to Sèvres. Samson copies are in hard paste, and Moritz Fischer at Herend in Hungary also used hard paste, to which he added the Sèvres mark.

There are also imitations of the earlier expensive styles, often the jewelled work. Painted medallion portraits of Louis XV and Madame du Barry are forgeries. They were not used in Sèvres painted decoration in the eighteenth century; although biscuit porcelain portraits exist. The date letter for 1761 is on some of this fraudulent ware.

There is a vast quantity of cheap, gaudy, meretricious hard paste china made in Paris that bears the name of Sèvres in auctioneers' catalogues and at dealers' who are not knowledgeable or not accurate in their assertions. The mark placed on this spurious Sèvres is the interlaced L's, frequently with the letter date A, which if genuine would represent 1753, the first year of the Sèvres factory as a royal business undertaking under the patronage of Louis XV, at which time it was producing a soft paste porcelain. Other letters used between the crossed L's are the initials of the decorators of the china. Thus C often stands not for 1755, but the name of Caile, a well-known painter of imitation Sèvres who worked in Paris in the early twentieth century; B. B. for Bareau and Bareau, a firm of decorators working at about the same time.

The minute paintings in reserves are frequently signed by such well-known names as Angelica Kauffmann, giving a beginner the notion that she herself had painted it, whereas it is a lithograph of a painting of hers, or even worse, a lithograph by someone else with her name attached to make the object more salable.

In examining Old Sèvres, special attention should be paid to the painting. If there has been any tampering or if the object is a forgery, this is where it will be most obvious. Genuine examples may be studied in museums, and for this there is no substitute.

XI

Other Important French Factories

Saint-Cloud (c. 1696–c. 1773 [?])

Little is known of early attempts to make porcelain in France. It is thought that a formula for an artificial porcelain was discovered at Saint-Cloud before 1700. The letters patent of 1696 granted by Louis XIV read "to the undertakers of the faience and porcelain works established at Saint-Cloud."

The contours of the ware were at first mainly of Chinese derivation. This was natural, since European porcelain makers, almost without exception, tried to reproduce both Oriental shapes and Oriental decoration in their effort to complete with the china imported from the East.

Saint-Cloud produced white pieces with modelled ornament inspired by the white ware of Fukien. Typical articles
have molded prunus blossoms and sprigs in relief accompanied with flowers, sprays, and rosettes on the surface. The
soft paste has a creamlike yellowish tinge. When chipped
or broken, the fracture shows a close, regular texture. The
glaze is clear and has very few bubbles. The articles most
commonly made are cups, saucers, jugs, teapots, coffeepots,
chocolate pots, coffee and chocolate services, trays, dishes,
plates, platters, tureens, sugar bowls, and tableware generally, knife handles, statuettes, grotesques, vases, bowls, and
flowerpots. The marks are carelessly used and are not certain
guides. A sun pressed into the paste was the first mark.
A later mark consisted of the letters S, C, in blue, with a
small cross above and the letter T underneath.

Chantilly (1725–1789)

A porcelain factory started at Chantilly about 1725 and
continued until the end of the eighteenth century. It was
under the protection of the Prince de Condé. The prince
was an eager collector of the lovely Japanese Imari ware,
which included excellent specimens with Kakiemon decoration, and pieces of Chantilly porcelain are largely copies
of this pattern. The design on Imari is usually based on
textile patterns, painted in an overcrowded manner in a
number of colors, of which a blackish dark blue and a
strong dark red predominate. It was first made about 1700
at Arita in Japan and named Imari because that was the
port from which it was shipped.

The body of Chantilly was a soft paste very much like
Saint-Cloud, although it seems to have been more solid
and stable in the firing. There were two distinct types of
glaze used at Chantilly. The one used during the first years

of the factory contained oxide of tin, which gave it a milky-white, opaque quality that enhanced the brilliancy of the decorations and increased its resemblance to the Japanese prototypes. Later, in order to meet the demands of competition with Sèvres and Mennecy-Villeroy, this glaze was abandoned and the factory adopted a transparent glaze.

 The usual mark used at Chantilly was a carefully drawn hunting horn applied in onglaze red. Late in the eighteenth century the same mark appears in blue accompanied by letters and figures meant to specify individual pieces.

Mennecy-Villeroy (1735–1773 or 1774)

The factory of Mennecy-Villeroy began in 1735 and continued until 1773–1774. The earliest pieces made at Mennecy were imitations of Saint-Cloud china. Somewhat later, the opaque tin glaze of Chantilly was used, and Chantilly wares were copied. In time, the factory developed a style of its own, although even then the output closely resembled Vincennes and Sèvres. The factory deserves special attention for its excellent artistic pieces modelled in the biscuit. Although it made some articles in the Chinese fashion, most of its products exhibit European contours. The decorative painting of this porcelain had bright reds, greens, yellows, and blues. All the usual types of wares made at other early French factories were made at Mennecy.

The mark consisted of the letters D.V. (signifying Duc de Villeroy). On the earlier work, this mark was painted in enamel color; later it was customary to scratch or engrave it on the paste before firing. On some of the Sèvres imita-

tions the two crossed L's of Sèvres are painted beside the
D.V. engraved in the body. Mennecy-Villeroy has been
forged in a hard paste ware complete with the D.V.
incised mark. The real thing is easily detected when you can
distinguish between hard and soft paste ware.

"Old Paris" Porcelain (1770–1850)

"Old Paris" is a term that describes the output of the many
factories that sprang up in and around Paris after 1770 when
hard paste porcelain was first introduced at Sèvres and the
various interdictions in favor of the royal factory were re-
laxed. Most of these factories were under the protection of a
member of the royal family or someone of equal importance.
They produced wares of a similar hard paste and glaze, and
there is a general similarity between the products that makes
them easily recognizable. For example, much was fairly
lavishly gilded with a brassy mercuric gilding that differs
considerably from early Sèvres. In the absence of a mark
it is almost impossible to differentiate among the factories,
and thus they are grouped together and called "Old Paris."
In many cases the china was obtained from Limoges or elsewhere and only decorated at the Paris *fabrique,* and the
mark, sometimes the name and address, is that of the decorator. The productions are in the Louis XVI or Empire
style until after 1814, when the surviving factories adopted
one or another of the styles current at the time. They produced dinnerware and the usual decorative items, vases,
mantel garnitures, and tea sets.

Old Paris is frequently found in shops, but the fact that
it is in great demand for interior decoration has made the
price higher than it rightfully deserves, since it is not always
of the quality to interest the serious collector.

There were a number of these factories, all producing

admirable wares with tasteful decoration. Following are some more deserving of attention and whose products are available.

FABRIQUE DE LA COURTILLE: This factory was started in 1773 in the rue Fontaine-au-Roy. It was first known as the Manufacture de Porcelaine Allemande, and its early ware is very German in style. The mark was a pair of crossed torches. It passed into the hands of Pouyat at Limoges in 1800.

FABRIQUE DU COMTE D'ARTOIS, FAUBOURG SAINT-DENIS: This was founded in 1770, and the letter H was registered for its mark. In 1779 it came under the protection of the Comte d'Artois, the King's brother (later Charles X) and used the mark C.P. under a coronet.

FABRIQUE DE LA RUE DE REUILLY, FAUBOURG SAINT-ANTOINE: The mark of this factory was an L in underglaze blue or else painted in gold on the glaze. Pieces of this work are rare, but they are of good quality and the decorations are well painted.

FABRIQUE DE CLIGNANCOURT: The factory was started in 1771 under the protection of the Comte de Provence (later Louis XVIII). The porcelain was of excellent quality. The first mark was that of a windmill, alluding to the nearby windmills of Montmartre, and later LSX in monogram. The letter D below a coronet has also been recorded.

FABRIQUE DE LA REINE, RUE THIROUX: A factory was founded in 1777 under the protection of Marie Antoinette. The products are still known as "porcelaine de la Reine." The mark is the letter A, with a crown above. Much of the decoration was small sprigs of cornflowers and the daisy. The rose was also a favorite. (See color insert, "Old Paris" cake plate.)

FABRIQUE DU DUC D'ANGOULÊME, RUE DE BONDY: This factory, founded in 1780, enjoyed the patronage of the Duc d'Angoulême, eldest son of the Comte d'Artois. It was founded by Dihl, and Guerhard was taken into partnership in 1786.

Before the Revolution, the pieces were marked G.A., which was occasionally set in an oval vignette with a coronet above it and painted in red or gold on the glaze. After the Revolution, the pieces were signed "Dihl" or "Guerhard and Dihl, Paris," the mark being applied in various ways.

FABRIQUE DE LA RUE POPINCOURT: This factory, which moved to the rue Popincourt in 1784, eventually became one of the largest porcelain factories in Paris. The painting was excellent. Flowers were widely used in decoration and ranged from strewn cornflowers to more elaborate mixed bouquets. The mark is usually "Nast à Paris" occasionally abbreviated to N.

FABRIQUE DU DUC D'ORLÉANS, RUE AMELOT: This factory came under the protection of the Duc d'Orléans in 1786, two years after its founding. The mark was an L.P.

Limoges-Haviland

Most people either own a piece of Haviland Limoges china or are familiar with the name. Grandmother was apt to have chosen a pattern of Haviland for her wedding china and ordered a large dinner set that included place settings for twenty-four or more, with numerous platters, vegetable dishes, pickle dishes, and berry bowls, enough to set a sumptuous table for a constantly growing family. In spite of the years that have passed since she received her wedding china and the constant use it received, numerable articles are still available.

The general term "Limoges" or "Haviland" is not adequate classification. There were many porcelain factories operating in Limoges, and "Haviland" comprises a father and two sons, who each had a separate factory.

The discovery of kaolin deposits at Saint-Yrieix around 1783 gave rise to the Limoges porcelain industry, although

Limoges-Haviland hard paste porcelain plate, c. 1850.

it was not until the nineteenth century that the great expansion of Limoges porcelain production took place. In 1783, Massie, Fourniera & Grellet were authorized to make hard paste porcelain at Limoges. In 1784 their factory was taken over by the King and served as a branch of Sèvres. Grellet managed the firm until 1788, when François Allaud succeeded him. The firm traded as Allaud during the first half of the nineteenth century; in 1886 it was taken over by Charles Field Haviland. A separate establishment continued under the name Pouyat and Allaud, which exists to the present day.

David Haviland was an American who became a naturalized Frenchman. He founded a factory at Limoges in 1842 for the manufacture of French porcelain for the American market, which effectively established the commercial success of Limoges. He employed industrial techniques and cheap effective means of decoration, such as chromolithography (introduced about 1875), as well as new procedures in overglaze and underglaze painting.

David Haviland died in 1879, and his sons soon started their separate concerns. Haviland & Co. was founded in 1892 by Charles Field Haviland for the manufacture of Limoges porcelain mainly for the American market. Theodore Haviland, brother of Charles, founded a rival hard paste porcelain factory also in 1892. Gas firing was introduced at Charles Field Haviland's factory in about 1900, with the result of a bigger production and increased shipments of china to America.

Other Limoges porcelain factories were:

M. Tharaud	c. 1827
Messrs Nenert & Rauault	c. 1831
Messrs Michel & Valin	c. 1834
Messrs Demartial & Talandier	c. 1867
Messrs P. Guerry & R. Delinières	c. 1867

The shapes and patterns of Limoges-Haviland china follow the Victorian styles favored by the American market during the middle of the nineteenth century. The output consisted mainly of table services. Decoration was mildly rococo with flowery naturalistic painting casually arranged. The Moss Rose pattern was most popular. The full palette colors were soft, noncommittal, melting into the substance of the hard glaze. The paste and glaze were perfect, the body being a pure white. Among the more important painters employed at the factories were Braquiemond, Boilvin, Dammouse, Delaplanche, and Ringel.

The earliest mark, used in the eighteenth century by Allaud, was CC impressed into the paste. The wares of the Haviland factories were usually clearly marked with the name "Haviland."

After 1891, the United States required that the country of manufacture appear on imported goods. It should be kept in mind that if the name of the country, in this case "France," accompanies the mark, the article was made after that date.

XII

English
Eighteenth-Century
Porcelain

English porcelain and pottery are more prevalent in the United States than ceramics from other countries, and the feasibility of being able to locate and acquire them convinces many a beginner-buyer to choose to collect them. There are many fields to choose from, including the products of the early English porcelain factories, earthenwares produced by Wedgwood and other eighteenth- and nineteenth-century potters, bone china from nineteenth-century factories, as well as Staffordshire figures and historic tablewares.

Usually the most difficult and expensive items to acquire are the eighteenth-century soft paste porcelains. Up to almost the middle of the eighteenth century, whatever experiments in porcleain making may have been conducted previously, there was no established china factory in England. The English knew and admired chinaware but depended upon the Orient, the soft paste products of France, or the hard paste china of Germany.

It is understandable that the English. procelain factories were later in getting started. Unlike Germany and France, where patronage of art was the custom, as in the case of Augustus II establishing the Meissen factory and the kings backing Sèvres, England did not grant its porcelain factories royal privileges; the initiative was confined to private commercial enterprises.

By far the greater part of the porcelain made in England during the eighteenth century was soft paste. It was made by the middle of the century at Chelsea, Bow, and Worcester, and soon after at many other factories. The formula for hard paste porcelain, reinvented, not bought or stolen from Germany, was achieved in 1768, too late to capture any significant place in the European market. When the formula for bone china was developed in 1794, the making of soft paste ceased, with the exception of a few examples at Nantgarw and Madeley.

Lovers of porcelain usually have a decided preference for either hard or soft paste. A collector of Chinese porcelain finds difficulty in understanding the soft paste imitation. Soft paste porcelain is fundamentally English; its very failings often make its appeal to the senses irresistible. There is something very restful about it that is lacking in its more glittering, polished, almost too-perfect relation.

It is important to remember that the translucence of soft paste was attained by mixing actual glass (or frit) in a powdered state with some form of white clay. The result was a material that is not resistant to any great degree of heat and which is easily scratched by a knife or file.

Chelsea Porcelain (1745–1784)

Chelsea was the first factory in England to make procelain, although at one time it was thought that Bow was. It is known that the Chelsea factory was working in London in or slightly before 1745 because the famous "goat-and-bee" jugs were produced with "Chelsea, 1745" scratched in the paste before it was fired—sufficient evidence that the factory was in existence and producing. About 1749, Nicholas Sprimont became manager, and from that time on, the main facts of Chelsea's history are known.

Sprimont was a silversmith from Liège, which resulted in his making jugs, saltcellars, and small vases based on silver models. He was also biased toward Continental styles, which, fortunately for the factory's success, were in great favor in England at that time.

The early porcelain of Chelsea may be divided into four main groups:

1. The first period, the 1740s, when incised triangle and raised anchor were used as marks.

2. The 1750s, marked with (at first) the raised anchor and then the red anchor drawn by the painter or gilder.

3. The 1760s, marked with a gold anchor.

4. The Chelsea-Derby period was from 1770 to 1784, when the anchor was used in conjunction with the letter D.

The early porcelain resembles milky-white glass, which by transmitted light (that is, when held against a strong electric light) shows tiny pin points of greater translucence. The glaze is very thick, glassy, sometimes ivory in tone, sometimes pure white because of the presence of tin oxide, and sometimes full of bubbles and tiny cracks. The factory mark was an incised triangle, rarely with a date. This is found on the goat-and-bee jugs—not to be confused with the reproduced goat-and-bee jugs made much later at the Coalport factory. On the latter the mark was scratched through the glaze and not incised into the unbaked body like the true early Chelsea. Examination with a magnifying glass will reveal the difference. A custom at Chelsea was to cover defects such as bubbles in the glaze or firing cracks with little painted leaves or insects. Gilding when used was very simple.

Though most Chelsea porcelain of the first and second periods was influenced by German and French fashions, the figures of birds with the mark of a raised anchor on an oval pad are an exception. The Meissen birds were modelled by Kändler from nature; the Chelsea modellers were inspired by the engravings in George Edwards' *History of Uncommon Birds*, with the result that they are stiff and formal in appearance.

The red anchor period was the best in the history of the factory, and the colors used in every kind of decoration were smooth and pastel-like with a sparing use of gilding. Among the desirables of this period are the plates painted with botanical, or "Hans Sloane," flowers. (Sloane [1660–1753] was a distinguished botanist.) The paste of this period is harder. Instead of pin points there are extratranslucent patches called "moons." The glaze is still thick and glassy, sometimes crackled, often black-spotted, but soft-looking.

The "Chelsea Toys," which were produced during the red anchor period, are the best known and most valuable of Chelsea productions. These were gems of modelling in the form of boxes, scent flasks, etuis, and trinkets of all kinds. Their outstanding features are the exquisite miniature painting and inscribed mottoes and messages in curious French.

The gold anchor period initiated the making of large figure groups, decorated with a riot of bright color, a profusion of gold, and elaborate rococo scrolling. The paste had fewer defects; the glaze was clear and glassy but often collected into thick, greenish, crazed pools in the hollows and crevices of figures. Domestic wares were inspired by Sèvres porcelain, and Sèvres's ground copies were copied. They included a strong claret known as rose Pompadour and *bleu de roi*, which was renamed "mazarine blue." These colors were used with painted reserves of exotic and naturalistic birds, fruit, flowers, Chinese figures, and figure subjects after Boucher and Watteau. Another decorative style of this period is the fine polychrome flower painting in conjunction with brilliant tooled gilding. The gold anchor denotes both the period and the decorative quality of the ware.

The gold anchor mark has been used fraudulently and extensively on hard paste porcelain made in France, not only on the better Samson wares but also on poor-quality figures of the late nineteenth and twentieth centuries. Many a tourist has been deceived by figures bearing a small gold anchor.

In 1770 the Chelsea factory was bought by William Duesbury of Derby, and this Chelsea-Derby period lasted until 1784, after which time all the work was conducted at the Derby factory. The mark consisted of the anchor of Chelsea joined with the D of Derby.

Articles made at Chelsea included an enormous variety. Besides table, tea, coffee, and chocolate services, the usual articles of household adornment, there were such frivolities as buttons, bottle stoppers, trinkets for watch chains, knobs for walking sticks, thimbles, smelling bottles, snuffboxes, and inkstands. There were dessert services with sweetmeat dishes in the form of artichokes, laurel leaves, sunflowers, and double leaves. Vegetable-shaped dishes, leaf-shaped dishes, and dishes made in the semblance of animals and birds were influenced by Meissen. Unlike other English soft paste porcelain factories, Chelsea produced very little underglaze-blue decoration.

Bow (1745–1776)

Although 1745 has been suggested as the beginning date of the Bow factory, there is no definite information of it before 1750. We do know that a patent was issued to Edward Heylyn and Thomas Frye in December 1744 and a second to Frye alone in 1749. It was in 1750, however, when the works belonged to Messrs. Crowther & Weatherby, that the first known piece of Bow china was made. It continued under their directorship until William Duesbury of Derby, with his insatiable acquisitive nature, bought the entire factory in 1776.

The products of the Bow factory held their own against the fanciful output of its neighboring rival, Chelsea, by being practical and useful. The factory produced blue-and-white, polychrome, and all-white wares. It made large services of a sturdy paste, stoutly potted, that was difficult to crack. Bow was influenced by Oriental blue-and-white, even calling the factory "New Canton." While Bow stressed the fact that its products were primarily useful as well as beautiful, it also made strictly ornamental ware, and there are Bow statuettes and groups.

All the porcelain produced at Bow was of a quality to command admiration. The body or paste of Bow is quite variable. The very early paste is not particularly white or translucent. It has a warm, creamy tint and is translucent where it is thin but opaque where it is thick. It is similar to early Chelsea, and it is possible that the formula of each was derived from a common source. Much of the later Bow

*Bow white soft paste porcelain figure
with bocage, c. 1755.*

paste is exceptionally hard (for soft paste), which is accounted for by the presence of bone ash.

The late pieces are better potted, thinner, and of whiter body. The early Bow glaze is rich in lead, shows a slightly yellowish tinge, and is apt to gather in the hollows of embossed patterns and at the bases of the pieces. The glaze of the late wares is harder and more brilliant. On the blue-and-white the glaze was often slightly tinted with blue, a device copied from the Chinese.

The decoration employed at Bow was influenced by both Oriental (Chinese and Japanese) and Continental (Meissen, Chantilly, Mennecy, and Sèvres) examples. The decorative processes included molding, piercing, modelling in relief, painting, transfer printing, and gilding. There are white pieces inspired by the white Fukien ware of China decorated with sprigs of prunus or plum blossoms in relief, and the earliest polychrome decoration was in the Kakiemon style or, as it was commonly called, the "Old Japan" pattern. Also in polychrome were wares embossed with flowers scattered at random, influenced by Meissen and Chantilly.

B

†

⚓

Large quantities of Bow china are unmarked, and on marked pieces various devices occur. The anchor and dagger, usually painted in red or a reddish brown, is important to remember. Sometimes there is an arrow, with or without an annulet; sometimes the monogram F.

Worcester (1751 to present)

The Worcester porcelain factory has continued in an unbroken line from the mid-eighteenth century to the present day, something that no other English factory can claim.

Since Worcester china has sustained its high quality, is perhaps the most easily recognized of all eighteenth-century English wares, and has no forgeries that are deceptive to the reasonably knowledgeable collector, it has always been greatly in demand and is still the most popular of all English wares.

Soapstone formed the basic substance of both Worcester and Bristol porcelain. Worcester began at Redcliffe Backs, Bristol, where Benjamin Lund, having a license to dig and search for soapstone, started to make porcelain in 1748. His factory was bought five years later by a partnership of business and other prominent local citizens of Worcester who wished to bring trade to their town, so the Bristol factory was moved to Worcester by the Severn River, where it had easy access to fuel supplies and transport to London, a hundred miles away. This factory showed its deep respect for Far Eastern porcelain by advertising itself as "The Worcester Tonquin Factory."

There were fifteen original subscribers to the company, the best known of them being Dr. John Wall and the manager, William Davis. This early period has in the past been termed the "Dr. Wall Period" but now is referred to as "First Period" Worcester, since it continued until 1783, seven years past Dr. Wall's death. In 1783 the factory was sold to Thomas Flight, and a new porcelain body and paste, which differed slightly from the old one, was introduced.

Worcester can make the claim that its glaze never crazed, which cannot be said for other eighteenth-century English porcelain. If an article is found crazed, it is an assurance it was not made at Worcester. Moreover, its teapots never cracked. Worcester made a denser body than Chelsea and Bow with better heat-resisting qualities. Often it followed Oriental models for shape and decoration, and its wares compared favorably with Chinese porcelain. In fact, early Worcester produced tableware so closely identical with the chinaware imported from the East that they advertised in the *Oxford Journal* in 1763 to inform the public that "services of Chinese porcelain can be made up with Worcester porcelain, so that the difference cannot be discovered." What they promised they were able to perform.

Worcester made a large amount of underglaze-blue-painted and -printed ware strongly influenced by Chinese prototypes. Many have molded forms, and there are tureens with dolphin knobs to the covers, jugs of various sizes formed of overlapping cabbage leaves, and some fitted with mask-shaped spouts. Tea services are fluted and ribbed. Outstanding among Worcester blue-painted wares are sauce boats molded with shell-, leaf-, basketwork, or scrolled motifs (with molded reserves bearing delicate Chinese landscapes and figure subjects), large hexagonal vases with domed covers, large lobed junket dishes, openwork baskets —oval or round, with or without handles, and with applied flower heads on the outside of the latticework intersections —two-handled sauce boats, caddy spoons, egg drainers (like caddy spoons but pierced), egg cups, mustard pots, little sweetmeat and pickle dishes in the form of leaves or shells, and feeding cups for babies or invalids. No gilding was ever used on the blue-painted wares.

Polychrome decoration was influenced by China, Meissen, and, after 1760, Sèvres. With the Sèvres influence predominant, Worcester reached its highest peak of decorative splendor. There are simpler, almost feminine festoons and arrangements of ribbons and trellises. At the other extreme are the famous "scale" grounds (influenced by fish-scale patterns) of blue, pink, and yellow, of which blue is by far the most common and on which panels were reserved and painted with Watteau-esque Chinese figures, exotic birds, and flowers. The reserves are usually outlined with gold scrolling. The same type of decoration is also often found in reserves on plain grounds of apple green, claret, yellow, and turquoise. (See color insert, Worcester bowl.)

The Worcester factory was justly proud of its transfer printing, for its quality has never been surpassed. Practically all the styles of painted decoration—fruits and flowers from nature, ceremonial and legendary subjects derived from K'ang-hsi, landscapes and scenes from literature, and domestic incidents—were imitated in the underglaze-blue transfer-printed wares. Transfer printing was first introduced at Worcester about 1756 with the employment of Robert Hancock, who discovered it. It naturally reduced the cost, and although early First Period Worcester pieces so decorated may be slightly less valuable, they are extremely attractive and worthwhile from the collector's point of view. Besides the blue-and-white, there are portraits, usually in black, such as one of the King of Prussia dated 1757. Floral patterns in overglaze enamel colors were done by 1760 with the aid of outline transfers.

Worcester rarely made figures. Only a few have been identified with certainty in recent years. Perhaps the most frequent survivors are a Turk and Companion and a Gardener and Companion.

Dr. Wall died in 1776, and Worcester's first period ended with the death of Davis, the manager, in 1783. The London agent, Thomas Flight, bought the business for his sons, Joseph and John, and the next years are known as the "Flight Period."

It may end some confusion to know that there were three separate porcelain factories in Worcester which added and subtracted partners and combined in various ways. In 1786, during Thomas Flight's time, Robert Chamberlain, a decorator who was first apprenticed to Dr. Wall, broke away from the Flight-Worcester factory and set up his own establishment in partnership with his brother Humphrey. At first he acquired china in the white from Flight and decorated it, but it was not long before he began to make his own porcelain. The first ware was a heavy gray, with a rippled surface to the glaze and a yellowish brown to the translucence, but this paste was experimental. By 1795 he had perfected a bone body and was producing the fine Regent china, although he also continued working in soft paste until 1815. Regent china is extremely white and translucent, and was reserved for use in important services and for the best decorative wares. Much of it has well-executed decorations of shells, feathers, and armorial designs. It is very collectible and should be sought after persistently, since good-quality nineteenth-century porcelain is becoming scarce.

The third offshoot of the original Worcester concern was founded in 1801 by Thomas Grainger, a nephew of Humphrey Chamberlain. His factory produced the new white, translucent bone-ash porcelain, but the decoration naturally differs very little from that found on the wares of the two larger factories. A characteristic feature is the presence of pale-pink harebells. It is fortunate that most Grainger ware, in common with that of the Flights and the Chamberlains, bears factory marks. It is noteworthy that it was the custom of all three factories to mark only a few pieces of a large service.

The following chart denotes names, manager-owners, or periods and working dates for easy reference:

C FIRST PERIOD (Dr. Wall) 1751–1783

C FLIGHT PERIOD 1783–1792

Flight 1788, Royal Patronage; crown used on most marks.

FLIGHT AND BARR (Thomas Barr) PERIOD
1792–1807

An incised B in the paste is often found on the base. Tea bowls have a double line on each flute.

BARR, FLIGHT AND BARR PERIOD 1807–1813
Mark: B.F.B.

FLIGHT, BARR & BARR PERIOD 1813–1840
Mark: F.B.B.

CHAMBERLAIN'S FACTORY 1786
Chamberlain bought Flight, Barr & Barr in 1840; Chamberlain Co. ended in 1852 and was bought by W. H. Kerr & R. W. Binns, who formed Worcester Porcelain Co. in 1840.

WORCESTER ROYAL PORCELAIN COMPANY
Founded in 1862.

THOMAS GRAINGER (painter at Chamberlain's)
Opened his factory in 1801.

GRAINGER & WOOD 1801–1812

GRAINGER, LEE & CO. 1812–1839
Called Grainger & Co. Son succeeded him and it continued until 1901.

WORCESTER ROYAL PORCELAIN CO. purchased Grainger & Co. in 1902. Continues to present day.

Caughley and Coalport Porcelain
(1772 to present)

Salopian (a term meaning Shropshire) porcelain, as it is often called, was made at Caughley (pronounced "Coffley") from 1772, and at nearby Coalport from 1814, until a few years ago when the works closed. Caughley owed its existence to a one-time Worcester apprentice, Thomas Turner. As was natural, he used the products of the Worcester factory as models, an inclination that was strengthened by the fact that in 1775 Robert Hancock, an engraver who had been at Worcester, also joined the factory.

Caughley porcelain is sometimes referred to as "the poor man's Worcester." The underglaze-blue-printed wares that were the factory's chief output are very like those produced at Worcester, though the steatitic paste of Caughley has a brownish translucence because the glaze was not blued with cobalt like Worcester's; neither did the glaze have Worcester's unmistakable glistening quality but was almost mat and often slightly pitted. There is also a violet tone to the underglaze blue that distinguishes it from Worcester, a characteristic that appeared after Turner returned from a visit to the French factories in 1780.

Turner introduced two extremely popular patterns, which have remained popular to the present day—the Willow and the Brosley Blue Dragon. The Willow pattern had no Chinese counterpart but was merely a crowded arrangement of many Chinese motifs. The famous legend attached to this design was invented to popularize the pattern. (According to the legend, Koon See, the daughter of a Chinese mandarin, refuses to submit to marriage to an old man as her father demands, for she already has her lover, Chang. The mandarin murders the young couple, whose souls are immediately transformed into blue doves, as on the Willow plate.) Other Caughley patterns printed in underglaze blue are the Fisherman, the Pheasant, and the Cornflowers.

The Caughley factory was purchased in 1799 by John Rose, a former apprentice of Turner's, and in 1814 he moved everything across the river to the factory at Coalport, which he already owned. Blue-and-white was still made for a few years, but Rose primarily produced ornate, richly colored styles. The Coalport bone paste and glaze is uniformly fine and whitely translucent. The Coalport pattern books, still in existence, show that the Coalport designers produced a large number of gaudy Japanese patterns in red, green, blue, and gold, but the majority of the designs were copies of Sèvres, with festoons and swags of flowers, urns, and many scrolled borders. Some fine bird painting was done in the Sèvres and Chelsea styles. These pieces were originally marked with an anchor and a letter C, both in blue, but sometimes are found with the authentic mark removed by acid and replaced by a misleading small gold anchor mark like Chelsea's.

The "raised flower" pieces of the 1820s are usually given the name of "Coalbrookdale." The applied flowers and leaves are always beautifully modelled and colored, though at times applied so lavishly that they obscure the lines and the surface nature of the porcelain. Most of this "Coalbrookdale ware" is unmarked, and it is not easy to distinguish from the very similar pieces made at Derby, Minton, Rockingham, and Chamberlain Worcester, particularly since each was using bone china and the same device of painting a landscape on one side of a vase or ornamental piece and a bouquet of flowers on the other.

To many connoisseurs the finest Coalport is that made from about 1850 onward, when the factory succeeded in improving its colored grounds, such as *bleu de roi*, turquoise, and rose Pompadour, so much that the wares were equal to the finest Sèvres.

The earliest Caughley mark was a crescent or letter C resembling the Worcester crescent; then the letter S, which

C

S

stands for "Salopian"; and later the word "Salopian" impressed in the paste, with sometimes the painted S or C mark used along with it. On Coalport the impressed marks "C. Dale" and CD in script are sometimes found.

Derby Porcelain (1750–1848, 1848 to present)

The Derby china factory was established by William Duesbury in 1755. Prior to that time Duesbury had been a china painter in London, executing commissions for Chelsea and Bow, now and then purchasing undecorated wares and painting them, or painting special pieces to the order of private customers. Little is known of Derby until 1770, when Duesbury bought the Chelsea factory; he kept both factories in operation until 1784, in the meantime buying the establishment at Bow. After 1784 all the work was conducted at the Derby factory.

Duesbury was a clever businessman and an able manager. When he died in 1786 he was succeeded by his son, the younger William Duesbury, who carried on the works until his death in 1795. The third William Duesbury and his step-father, Michael Kean, then conducted the business, which was known as Duesbury and Kean. This partnership was dissolved in 1811, and the business was sold to Robert Bloor. The commercially minded Bloor revoked the standards that had prevailed previously, and the business of this formerly prosperous factory fell off considerably. By 1848 it was closed. A small factory soon started up again, run by a group of former Derby workmen, with a Mr. Locker as manager. Later proprietors of this venture were Stevenson and Hancock. From its rebirth, the factory succeeded and continues to the present day. In 1876 a new and altogether distinct company was formed, which is known as the Royal Crown Derby Porcelain Company.

The most splendid era of Derby decoration of domestic wares began when the Chelsea factory was taken over in 1770. With the aid of artists and chemists who left London to join him, Duesbury was able to produce patterns that set a standard for all the English factories, with the possible exception of Worcester. Derby developed lovely ground colors of claret and turquoise—although not of Chelsea excellence—and a lapis lazuli, known to collectors as "Derby blue," or "Smith's blue," which replaced the Chelsea dark blue. There is a profusion of festoons and swags, scattered detached flower sprays, urns, and classical figures in gray or crimson monochrome, and a variety of striped and wavy patterns, of which the gold stripes are best known.

During the period 1784 to 1810, when the well-known mark of crown and crossed batons was used, many specialist artists worked on services and cabinet pieces. They painted in an almost miniature style on ground colors of yellow, pale red, fawn, pink, claret, and turquoise. Also produced at this time in soft paste were the handsome "Japan" patterns, now called "Imari." The artists had an excellent paste to work on. It was white and translucent, though it had an unfortunate tendency to craze. (See color insert, Derby shaped dish.)

Bloor's managership in 1811 brought an artistic decline, but the new bone-ash paste was introduced and some good pieces were produced. The decoration was mediocre by Derby standards.

Derby produced very fine figures, many from Chelsea molds. The collector should beware two pitfalls in purchasing Derby figures. First, there are on the market many specimens, some of them of large size, made by the notorious Samson of Paris, complete with marks that are much too boldly drawn. On the surface, they are very much like the true Derby, but their hard paste body is obvious. Second, other figures, replicas and not forgeries, were made at Derby by Stevenson and Hancock between 1850 and 1870. Their late origin is shown by the presence of the letters S

and H on either side of the crown and crossed batons.
These should not get the high prices the earlier figures do.

The earliest Derby mark was a script D, but
it is very rare. The usual mark is a D beneath a
crown, which was used to about 1782. It was
usually applied in underglaze blue, but is also
found in purple, green, and rose. Not long
after 1782 crossed batons and six dots accompanied the crowned D. This mark is usually in
purple or mauve, though it may occur in red,
blue, or gold. While Kean was a partner, the
letter K is occasionally found with the D.
When Bloor bought the works, the pieces were
marked "Bloor, Derby," with or without the
crown. The Bloor marks were generally
printed. A gothic D, crowned and printed in
red, dates to the Bloor period. Forged Meissen
and Sèvres marks in underglaze blue occasionally appear on Derby pieces.

Longton Hall Porcelain (1750–1760)

For many years little was known about this factory, and
attributions were almost entirely conjecture, based on
slight evidence. The discoveries of Dr. Bernard Watney,
both those of a documentary nature and those arising from
excavation on the site, have turned this into one of the best
documented of the smaller English factories.

The factory was founded by William Littler, a salt-glaze
stoneware potter. (Some of the Longton Hall soft paste
porcelain productions closely resemble existing specimens
of salt-glazed ware.) Figures were made here from the very
beginning. The earliest ones belong to the group that has

been given the descriptive name of "snowman." They were similar to ones made in salt glaze by Thomas Whieldon. Over thirty models have been identified. The modelling is so poor as to suggest that difficulty was encountered in working with a noncoherent soft paste. Most are hollow. Their unglazed bases are pierced with small conical holes, while in places the thick, glassy glaze has either failed to adhere to the paste or else has collected in blobs.

The figures improved in a few years and achieved equality as far as detailed modelling to those made at Chelsea, although they were usually decorated with very bright, strong enamels, a thick brown, a strong pink, dark blue, and yellowish green. The cheeks of faces were reddened, as at Derby.

Littler was the inventor of a remarkable opaque blue enamel, which is now called "Littler's blue." Some of the leaf forms of the early domestic wares, such as sauce boats and pickle trays, are covered with this vivid, mottled color, but it has long since disappeared. Raised white enamel was sometimes used as an alternative to gilding.

After 1757 domestic wares improved and became more elegant, with intricate molding of strawberries, leaf forms, and an occasional openwork rim. Some of the finest decoration found on Longton Hall is done by John Haymens, a painter referred to for convenience as the "Castle Painter."

The Longton Hall china factory was closed when the entire stock was sold in 1758. It is possible that some of these were unfinished articles, which could explain why many a piece that would otherwise pass as Longton Hall is not identified as such because the decoration on it is not typical of the factory. These may have been bought in the white and decorated by another factory.

Longton Hall china was seldom marked and may easily be mistaken for inferior Bow or Chelsea ware. When marked, it had two L's crossed or a device evolved from two L's.

Lowestoft China (c. 1757–c. 1802)

Lowestoft, the town whose name has been falsely given to the hard paste porcelain made in China and exported by the Chinese to Europe and America, is in Suffolk, England, and with Worcester and Caughley is one of the three provincial towns that produced porcelain. They all catered to ordinary people and produced useful wares.

The china factory at Lowestoft was first proposed in 1756, but it was 1757 before a company was formed and succeeded in producing a salable porcelain from a formula provided by Robert Browne, who possibly obtained it from Bow. The soft paste, containing bone ash in much the same proportions, is very similar to that at Bow, and specimens decorated in underglaze blue are often difficult to differentiate from those made at the London factory. Like Bow, the degree of translucence by transmitted light is variable. The majority of existing Lowestoft porcelain is decorated in both painted and printed underglaze blue. The earlier productions were influenced by Worcester, as evidenced by the patterns employed, and by the use of the Worcester crescent mark, which appears frequently. In contrast to Worcester, Lowestoft wares are thicker and not as neatly potted, and the greenish or bluish glaze is full of minute bubbles. Lowestoft is naïve and slightly primitive. Inscribed wares are important. These often bear the name of the owner as well as the date and the words "A Trifle from Lowestoft." Also in this group are birth tablets, which record the name and birth of a child. Since Lowestoft produced charming little dolls' tea sets, the word "toylike" can aptly describe their products.

The use of enamel colors commenced about 1770. A mauve pink is fairly peculiar to the factory. This was used with patterns copied from the Chinese Mandarin decoration after 1775. Only a few figures were made at Lowestoft, *putti* and small animals.

There appears to have been no regular factory mark on the Lowestoft china, and many pieces have no mark of any kind. Marks of other factories were now and again copied. Comparing the marks of blue-painted wares: Worcester's workmen's marks were used as alternatives to the factory marks, at Bow the artists' numerals were usually placed near the center of the bases, whereas at Lowestoft, the workmen's numerals, commonly ranging from 1 to 30, are found close to the foot rim.

Liverpool Porcelain Factories (1756–c. 1780)

Liverpool was one of the big centers for delft making in England during the mid-eighteenth century, and it would have been strange had the Liverpool potters not tried to make the translucent ware that was becoming so popular. By the last half of the eighteenth century, several factories in the city were producing porcelain. For a long time the term "Liverpool" has been misused to describe any porcelain which has uncertain identification. In the past there was little evidence to show that porcelain was made in Liverpool during the eighteenth century, but recently it has been discovered several factories were making it.

The first porcelain maker in Liverpool of which there is any knowledge was Robert Podmore, a potter from the Worcester works, who in 1755 entered into an agreement with Richard Chaffers and Philip Christian. They made a soapstone porcelain similar to Worcester's with a formula produced by Podmore. Chaffers' porcelain has many resemblances to Worcester's—the body is grayish and the glaze is slightly blued. When Chaffers died in 1765, the factory passed to Christian, who continued running it until 1776. Other factories that opened there during this period were Reid & Co., Samuel Gilbody, William Ball, Zachariah Barns & Cotter, James & John Pennington, Seth Pennington, and Thomas Wolfe.

During the Chaffers period, shapes and moldings aped the Worcester designs. A singular characteristic of Liverpool is a handle that is either cloven or shaped like a snake's head where it grips the rim of the vessel. When Christian took over after Chaffers' death, he gradually discarded the soapstone body and replaced it with a bone-ash one. The result was a bluish-white paste instead of one inclined toward gray. The glaze is a dirty bluish color and tends to collect behind foot rims.

Blue-painted designs were direct copies of Worcester, though there are one or two exceptions. One found nowhere else features a slender double-trunked palm tree standing before a fence which disappears on the right behind what seems to be five upright boards surmounted by a peony. This design, like others painted at Liverpool, had a simple trellis border.

There are no certain marks attributed to eighteenth-century Liverpool porcelain factories, although "Christian" impressed in the paste is recorded.

English True Porcelain Factories

(Plymouth 1768–1770, Bristol 1770–1781, New Hall 1781–1825)

English porcelain potters seemed content to continue making artificial or soft paste porcelain. No effort was made by the early factories to seek the formula for true

*Pair of Plymouth-Bristol hard paste
porcelain candlesticks, c. 1770.*

or hard paste porcelain as the Continental potters did. It was not until 1768 that William Cookworthy opened at Coxide, Plymouth, Devonshire, a factory for the manufacture of true porcelain in the Chinese manner. It is possible that Cookworthy was informed of the ingredients of true porcelain by Andrew Duché, a porcelain maker from Savannah, Georgia, who was the first English-speaking person to successfully make a hard paste porcelain, which he manufactured in Savannah from 1738 to 1743. He went to England to seek assistance in continuing his factory, and during this visit had an introduction to Cookworthy.

The early wares of the Plymouth factory are often primitive and inclined to show many manufacturing faults. The glaze is variable in thickness, often speckled, sometimes with a slightly pitted surface resembling the effect that the Chinese describe as "chicken skin." Flatware is scarce, which points to difficulties in potting. The most frequent survivals are leaf-shaped pickle trays, sauce boats (patterned after silver), mugs—baluster-shaped and straight-sided—and teapots and coffeepots.

Shellwork was a common form of decoration, and a shell (to hold salt) mounted on a pile of small shells and coral was very common. Decoration in painted underglaze blue was often used, the blue usually blackish in tone. Practically no transfer printing in underglaze blue was done.

In 1772 Richard Champion was licensed by Cookworthy to manufacture under his license at Bristol, and in 1774 Cookworthy assigned his patent to him and transferred the Plymouth factory to Bristol, and the ware is thereafter termed "Bristol."

The style of Plymouth-Bristol porcelain began to change with Champion's participation. Tea services were made, and cups and saucers are the most frequently surviving articles of Bristol. These had not been made successfully at the Plymouth factory. Vases were produced in considerable quantity. These had masks on either side and were decorated with well-modelled applied flowers. Many were hexagonal. Excellent floral and bird enamelled painting decorates much of the production. Well-modelled figures were produced, influenced by the work at Derby. Underglaze-blue decoration is rare, and transfer printing has been found on only a couple of articles. (See color insert, Plymouth-Bristol vase.)

Although there were imperfections in the Plymouth glaze, the difficulties were overcome at Bristol. An evenly distributed, clear, brilliant glaze was produced. The simpler ware was glazed and fired at one operation, in the Chinese manner. The more elaborate pieces were first fired to a partial biscuit state, then dipped in the glaze and fully fired. A certain amount of porcelain, sparsely and simply decorated in sprig and similar designs, was made to supply a cheaper market, probably to compete with Wedgwood's creamware. This often is referred to as "cottage Bristol."

Plymouth and Bristol porcelain are very scarce. Of the Plymouth items found for sale, the large bell mugs painted with birds in enamel colors bring the highest prices. There are many inferior specimens of Plymouth porcelain, which is to be expected from a factory whose work was largely experimental. Plymouth was short-lived, and even the cruder pieces are scarce and costly. Bristol porcelain is also expensive, especially fine sets in reasonably complete condition.

When Plymouth is marked, it sometimes carries the alchemical symbol for tin, which looks like a combination of the Arabic numerals 2 and 4. On the blue-and-white pieces, the mark is in underglaze blue; on the polychrome pieces, it is in red or reddish brown. The regular Bristol mark was a cross, incised in the paste, in blue underglaze, or on the glaze in gold. The mark B was also used.

When Richard Champion brought the Bristol china works to an end, he transferred the patent rights to a group of experienced potters, who, in 1781, established a factory in Tunstall. In 1782 they moved the establishment to New Hall, at Shelton, and made true, or hard paste, porcelain there until 1810, when the factory went into the production of bone china.

New Hall produced simple wares in true porcelain, usually with a decoration of floral sprays or copies of simple scenes based on contemporary Chinese Export porcelain (novices, in fact, often find difficulty in distinguishing between the two). The elaborate Cantonese Mandarin patterns were copied. It is comparatively easy to find New Hall tea bowls and saucers; the more important pieces—teapots and cream jugs, for instance—are much scarcer. The present market is getting a fairly high price for New Hall.

New Hall china is not always marked. The earliest mark was the letter N incised in the paste; also a script N in red. A later mark used the name "New Hall" in italics in a double circle, transfer-printed on the glaze. The majority of the pieces are marked with the pattern numbers.

It is a great satisfaction to be able to make a correct identification of an article of eighteenth-century English porcelain, but there are many other detections that bring us much pleasure.

XIII

Wedgwood
and His Followers

Josiah Wedgwood (1730–1795);
  Wedgwood (1795 to present)

English art and decoration were dominated by the spirit
of the classic revival during the second half of the eighteenth
century. Josiah Wedgwood exemplified that spirit in ceramics in the same way the Adam brothers did in architecture
and decoration. Wedgwood became principally involved
with the classical styles we associate with his name around
1768. He was directly inspired by the illustrations of the
Etruscan collection of Sir William Hamilton, English Ambassador at Naples between 1764 and 1800, in his cata-

logues published in 1766–1767. He drew his models from this publication, working in black basalt and various colored jaspers to produce such perfect copies that it is often difficult to tell the classical Wedgwood wares from the true antiquities of Etruria, Greece, and Rome.

Prior to this, however, Wedgwood had been working as a potter, experimenting and improving methods of potting in Staffordshire—a district ten miles long that comprised Stoke-on-Trent, Hanley, Cobridge, Etruria, Burslem, Fenton, Tunstall, Longport, Shelton, and Lane End and that was called "The Potteries." The period 1720 to 1740 was a transitional one in Staffordshire, one in which a great field of pioneer workers experimented with clays and glazes and made amazing technical advances. This period was succeeded (1740–1780) by a renaissance of earthenware in England that established the reputation of Staffordshire.

It was in this stimulative atmosphere that Wedgwood began his illustrious career as a potter, at age eleven. At that time he was apprenticed to his elder brother, Thomas, as a thrower (a shaper of round articles on a revolving wheel), at a pottery at Churchyard Works, Burslem. He worked there, learning the various stages of potting, until 1754, when he entered his first partnership. It was with Thomas Whieldon, who had a small potworks at Fenton Vivian. Whieldon was a highly talented craftsman producing marbled and black Egyptian wares and plates and tea articles of tortoise shell. His productions were the finest Staffordshire of the mid-eighteenth century. Wedgwood perfected his knowledge of the earthenware being made by Whieldon, experimented, and made new discoveries.

Wedgwood's most important invention during this period was (as described by him in his Experiment Book for March 24, 1759) "green glaze, to be laid on common white

First Period Worcester soft paste porcelain bowl,
scale blue ground with reserves of exotic birds
outlined with rococo gold scrolling, c. 1780.

"Old Paris" hard paste porcelain cake plate, rue Thiroux (Fabrique de la Reine), c. 1815.

Chinese Export porcelain plate, Rose Medallion pattern, c. 1825.

Plymouth-Bristol hard paste
porcelain vase, c. 1775.

Meissen porcelain figure, c. 1825.

*Wedgwood pearlware dish
of a lustred modelled shell, c. 1790.*

English bone china plate, c. 1825.

Tucker hard paste porcelain plate, American, c. 1830.

Bloor Derby shaped dish,
Japan pattern, c. 1815.

*Pair of Pratt ware pottery
miniature dishes, c. 1785.*

(or cream-color) biscuit ware. Very good." This green glaze was especially well suited for cauliflower and pineapple models. Of equal importance was the discovery of a yellow glaze recorded in Wedgwood's Experiment Book in 1760. Wedgwood employed these early improvements and inventions both before he left Whieldon and after he established his own works at Ivy House in 1759 (at which time he became a master potter), and it is impossible to tell which were made at which place. All of this early colored glaze is therefore referred to as "Whieldon-Wedgwood" and was made during the years 1754–1764, which include the Whieldon-Wedgwood partnership at Fenton Vivian from 1754 to 1759, followed by the Ivy House Works period, from 1759 to 1764.

About 1760 Wedgwood perfected a cream-colored earthenware similar to one already being manufactured by other Staffordshire potters. He produced a number of articles in it and presented them to Queen Charlotte, wife of George III, calling it "Queen's Ware," a name it bears to the present day. Because of its lightness and elegance, cream-colored earthenware became the most fashionable type of utility pottery. Until its appearance, porcelain was considered the only material suitable for drinking tea, but with this new refinement of the paste, creamware came into demand for tea equipage.

When left plain or undecorated, Wedgwood's creamware relied chiefly on its classical symmetry of form for artistic merit. The cut and pierced designs and many other shapes followed those of the silversmith. In dessert dishes and centerpieces, the beauty was in the modelling, a style closely followed by the Leeds potters, who also made excellent creamware.

Decorated Queen's Ware was of two types—either painted in enamel colors, or transfer-printed in red, puce, or black. This last was a new style of printing by Sadler and Green of Liverpool, and Wedgwood periodically sent his wares to them to be decorated.

Wedgwood did not use the cream-colored body strictly for domestic wares. Among his many productions, Wedgwood made some fine colored figures, remarkable for strong modelling and subdued in coloring. These include large figures of Fortitude, Charity, Ceres, and Juno, among others. He also made many small colored creamware busts, typical examples being those of Rousseau and Voltaire.

In 1775, Wedgwood's continuing experiments to produce creamware with a whiter body and glaze resulted in a fine earthenware that he termed "Pearlware." Its glaze is white or bluish in appearance. It was later extensively manufactured in Staffordshire and Leeds, being an ideal body for the very popular underglaze-blue-transfer-printed articles made by so many potters during the early part of the nineteenth century. The most notable productions of Wedgwood in this whiter ware are the dessert services of lustered modelled shells. (See color insert, Wedgwood dish.)

Wedgwood's greatest triumph in ceramic art was the accomplishment of an endless variety of shapes that he termed "ornamental," to distinguish them from Queen's Ware or other useful earthenware. By 1768 he had invented a fine black body, called basalt. It had nearly the same properties as the natural basalt, the Egyptian marble for which it was named. It resists acids, withstands heat, and takes a high polish. He used it frequently, along with (a little later) his jasper ware, for copies of classical vases and plaques. By the time he moved to his new factory at Etruria in 1759, he was making vases with red encaustic painting on the black and calling them "Etruscan" vases.

Continuing in the spirit of classicism, Wedgwood began in 1773 to experiment with a jasper body, which he succeeded in perfecting about 1775. This is a hard, fine-grained

*Wedgwood blue jasper sugar bowl
with raised white classical figures, c. 1785.*

stoneware, which he referred to as "biscuit porcelain," as he termed his basalt "black porcelain." Wedgwood's jasper ware is of various colors—blue in differing tones, sage green, olive green, lilac, pink, yellow, black, and white, its natural color without the addition of metallic oxides for coloring. It is usually made with white relief on a single color, but is also produced in three colors, termed "tri-color jasper." This is rarer, and it demands a very high price. Jasper was mainly used for products of highly ornamental character; however, it was also produced in utilitarian objects, such as tea and coffee services, dishes, and flower vases. The plaques made from jasper were used in interior decoration as well as for shoe buckles and portrait medallions.

Wedgwood's classic subjects were not unimportant copies of ancient art but were executed from designs by a band of good artists working together and steeped in the spirit of the new classical revival. John Flaxman, James Tassie, John Bacon, William Hackwood, Thomas Stothard, George Stubbs, and William Greatbach were all employed by Wedgwood. Distinguished amateurs such as Lady Diana Beauclerk and Lady Templeton also supplied him with designs.

It was during this classical period that Wedgwood had as his partner Thomas Bentley, a man of wide culture, possessing a knowledge of classical and Renaissance art. Bentley was also a great linguist, which aided Wedgwood in marketing his wares all over the world.

Because of its success with earthenware, the Wedgwood factory continued to produce only that until 1812. Then, for ten years—from 1812 to 1822—it put out a bone china, much of it as fine as any that can be found. The production of bone ceased after 1822, and it was not until 1878 that its manufacture was resumed. It continues to be made in ever-popular patterns.

It is often thought that all Wedgwood is marked. The colored glazed ware of the Whieldon-Wedgwood period is not marked, and neither is some of his other early ware. It is impossible at times to be certain whether creamware is his or the work of one of his contemporary imitators, who copied not only his creamware but also his basalts and jasper. The results in creamware were sometimes, as in the case of Elijah Mayer and Leeds Pottery, not inferior to Wedgwood's.

Unmarked pieces of Wedgwood should not be neglected because they do not bear a mark. Many articles of fine quality are at times without one. This may be for various reasons: carelessness, putting the piece to the lathe after marking, thinning down medallions, or perhaps the lapidary's work grinding it to fit a metal mount. Marks are only one of the facts to consider in dating a piece of Wedgwood. Other factors—such as design, body technique, numbers, and various symbols—must be considered in each case.

"Wedgwood" in either capital or lower case letters, impressed with printer's type in varying sizes, is on the majority of pieces, although it does not give an idea of the date since this mark has been used continuously from the eighteenth century to the present day. In 1891, when the McKinley Tariff Act required the country of origin to be named on all objects for the American market, the word "England" was added to "Wedgwood." However, if a piece was intended for the home market, it would not have it. In the twentieth century, "Made in England" instead of just "England" is placed on articles.

This mark was continued by Josiah Wedgwood's early successors, except on the porcelain made between 1812 and 1816, when the name was printed in red, blue, or gold. The impressed name with the addition of three capital letters—

symbols for month, workman, and year—was introduced in 1860 and ran until 1930. Between 1842 and 1882, a diamond-shaped registry mark was used, as it was by many manufacturers. It is an indication that the design was registered with the British Patent Office; earthenware and glass was Class IV, as indicated in the topmost section of the mark. Where the manufacturer's name does not appear in addition to the mark, it is possible to determine the date by checking the date letters. Beginning in 1878 bone china was printed with a representation of the Portland Vase above three stars and the word "Wedgwood," which developed into the present vase mark on bone.

The present mark printed on Queen's Ware is WEDG-WOOD OF ETRURIA AND BARLASTON in the form of a circular stamp, the name on the axis, with MADE IN ENGLAND in microscopic letters below it. This mark was adopted in 1940.

There are varying forms of circular stamps with WEDG-WOOD & BENTLEY in capital letters, with or without the word ETRURIA, or WEDGWOOD & BENTLEY in two lines or forming an oval. The various WEDGWOOD & BENTLEY marks are the only ones that give exact evidence of manufacture between 1769 and 1780, the time of Wedgwood's partnership with Bentley.

The Wedgwood mark was forged or imitated in the eighteenth and the nineteenth centuries by various potters. Some good-quality creamware and blue-and-white jasper medallions are marked "Wedgwood & Co." These were made by Ralph Wedgwood & Co. before 1796, or later by Tomlinson, Foster, Wedgwood & Co. This mark was not used after 1801. WEDGWOOD & CO. LTD., impressed, was a fraudulent mark employed after 1900. Also fraudulent are WEDGEWOOD (with use of second E), WEDG-WOOD, and various others.

Contemporaries and Followers of Wedgwood

Josiah Wedgwood had the inspiration to transpose classic
ornament into Staffordshire pottery. A school of potters
developed around this idea, such men as William Adams,
John Turner, Elijah Mayer, and Henry Palmer of Hanley,
who, aside from being competitors, produced work equal
and at times finer than the master's.

William Adams of Greengates (1745–1905), in a family
renowned for its potters, produced, among other fine earthenwares, the beautiful Adams blue jasper, its violet tone
distinguishing it from Wedgwood's blue jasper. His finely
modelled classic reliefs are less frigid than Wedgwood's,
since he drew his inspiration more from Latin than from
Greek models. As a rule, Adams' jasper is a bit more waxen
than that of Wedgwood, but never shiny. He was an exceptional modeller and designed himself several of his
finest pieces, such as the Seasons, Venus Bound, Cupid
Disarmed, Pandora, Psyche Trying One of Cupid's Darts,
and the Muses. His stoneware jugs with reliefs of hunting
scenes are often mounted in silver and can be dated accurately by the silver marks.

The usual mark found is ADAMS, impressed on the bottom. Occasionally the mark is ADAMS & CO. About 1815 his
son, Benjamin Adams, used the impressed mark B. ADAMS,
which appears on stoneware and on underglaze-blue-printed
pearlware. Not all Adams was marked.

John Turner, of Lane End (1739–1787), was an intimate
friend and neighbor of Wedgwood's as well as a rival potter.
He made remarkably fine jasper, which differed from Wedg-

.wood's in that the body was more closely related to porcelain. He was an accomplished modeller himself and, following the Greek school in design, produced well-proportioned articles. His unglazed stoneware surpassed anything that his contemporaries achieved. Working with a perfect clay that he found in his own neighborhood, he was capable of modelling jugs with exact, fine, sharp designs in relief. He set a new fashion with his classic reliefs and also deviated from the classical by modelling figures in old English costume engaged in archery and other homelier subjects. Often these mugs and jugs had silver rims and covers. Turner made a fine-quality black basalt, preferred by some to Wedgwood's.

Turner was the first Staffordshire potter to use underglaze-blue printing. These wares frequently have perforated borders. He also produced creamware and an excellent-quality earthenware with rich ground colors and enamelled painting.

After John Turner's death in 1787, the pottery was continued by his sons, John and William, until 1804, when John withdrew from the partnership. They continued the staple lines of their father, but business declined and they remained steadily in debt. In January 1800 they patented a new type of hard, durable opaque earthenware, the forerunner of ironstone china. This new body was used for dessert services and other useful wares, always neatly potted and often decorated with brilliant "Japan" patterns. These articles bear the painted mark "Turner's Patent," but they are rare. It is recorded, but not proved, that Josiah Spode purchased the patent rights about 1805 and renamed the body "Stone China." Most marked Turner bears the name TURNER, or TURNER & CO. This latter mark was probably used from 1780 to 1786 and from 1803 to 1806. The mark TURNER & ABBOTT (Turner's partner on the Continent) is recorded from 1783 to 1787, but it is very rare.

All Turner wares are of good quality and are collectible items.

The potters mentioned above, although influenced by Wedgwood, were not imitators. They showed their own innovations in body and design. Henry Palmer of Hanley is in a different category. He showed a spark of originality by anticipating Wedgwood by some five years in applying bas-reliefs to his black vases and by his sprinkled marbled ware touched with gold, but these two productions ended his ingenuity. He was a great trial to Wedgwood, as it is said he procured every new pattern of his on its appearance and copied it.

Collectors, as did Wedgwood, acknowledge the fine quality of the work of Palmer and his partner, J. Neale, who was taken in when financial difficulties caused failure in 1778. This is understandable when one examines a piece of Palmer and Neale's jasper or basalt, since it will reveal an amazing mastery of technique. It is finely potted and well balanced in ornament and design. If it were not for the impressed mark, these jasper vases might pass for Wedgwood.

The wares were marked H. PALMER or PALMER. HANLEY was the earliest mark used. Sometimes only the initials H.P. were used. The mark NEALE alone is found, and often NEALE & CO. These marks are usually in circles; one article bears the mark I. NEALE, with the word HANLY (spelled wrong) beneath. About 1788 Robert Wilson joined the firm, and after this date his name alone appears.

Elijah Mayer (1770–1813) produced black basalt tea wares from about 1786. His fine teapots bearing a seated woman as a finial to the lid are well known. (Since other factories producing black basalt often used this same finial, it cannot be considered for attribution.) His unglazed cane-colored ware bore simple decorations of lines in green and blue. His productions are often attributed by beginners to Turner, since there is a similarity. The mark impressed is E. MAYER, and after 1820 E. MAYER & SON. Beginning in 1845 the mark was JOSEPH MAYER and JOSEPH MAYER & CO.

As the eighteenth century drew to a close, Wedgwood's influence became more and more removed. Nevertheless, some traces and forms continued. This is seen particularly in black basalt teapots and coffeepots, buff-colored stoneware, and jugs with sporting and classic subjects in relief. However, in creamware, the most produced of English earthenwares, the forms and ornamentation quickly changed from the styles of Wedgwood's Queen's Ware. Creamware jugs and mugs provided a wide range of the potter's fancy in political, satirical, patriotic, humorous, and fancy subjects.

There were many factories, nearly one hundred, producing in the Staffordshire district alone, and by 1800 over fifty thousand people were employed in The Potteries. Little wonder that it is often impossible to pinpoint where an article was made. Many factories worked in the same paste and used the same designs. Designers, painters, and workmen shifted from factory to factory and carried their secrets and individual ideas with them. Let it be sufficient, until more knowledge is acquired, to be able to judge the quality and approximate age of an article of late-eighteenth- and early-nineteenth-century English pottery. Time and experience will bring the aptitude to make a more accurate attribution.

XIV

Other Outstanding English Potters

Leeds Pottery (c. 1760–1820)

Leeds pottery is one of the most sought-after of English earthenwares and one of the most difficult to find. However, when found and obtained it gives intense satisfaction. Its fame is based mainly on its fine creamware, which was produced from about 1783 to about 1800. Leeds produced other wares, such as red earthenware, white salt-glazed stoneware, red stoneware, and pearlware, but it is the cream-colored earthenware, both plain and decorated, that was the important product of Leeds. It was made at first as an imitation of Wedgwood's Queen's Ware, then the firm of Hartley,

Greens & Co., of Leeds, improved the method of manufacture to such an extent that it actually surpassed its rivals, especially the objects patterned with perforations.

Creamware was decorated in many ways. The early uncolored Leeds in rococo and classical shapes depended on its gracious design, fine form, good proportion, and sometimes molded decoration for its appeal. Many of the Leeds forms and decorations were derived from the designs of the silversmith. Full use was made of pierced openwork decoration, in which the Leeds pottery excelled. Aside from its beauty, the openwork decoration served another purpose. Openwork pieces were lighter in weight than the solid ware, and, with the large demand on the Continent for creamware, which was taxed according to weight, Leeds paid less in taxes than its English rivals.

This perforated ware, following metalworking technique, was cut sharply and clearly—diamonds, hearts, circles, and so on—shape by shape with a simple hand punch, while the unfired clay was "leather hard." Wedgwood copied the idea, using block punches, which eliminated even the slight unevenness of the hand-cut article.

The Leeds factory turned out, among other things, large centerpieces, more than two feet high, of complex design and intricate molded decoration, made in several parts and complete with removable baskets and bottles; urns with refined and complicated modelling, made to be used as candelabra; elaborately designed tureens, cockle pots, and potpourris, often encircled with figures. These ambitious productions testify to the marvelous proficiency of the Leeds potters. Many of the designs can be found in the *Leeds Pattern Book*.

Leeds creamware, when colored, has either enamelled or transfer-printed decorations. As a rule brick red and black predominated in the enamelled colors, but also a wide range of green, blue, purple, rose, and yellow were used, occasionally touched with gilding. The enamelled ware consists of teapots, coffeepots, cups and saucers, plates, sugar bowls, slop bowls, tea canisters, mugs and jugs, and sometimes little screw-top boxes used for snuff, patches, or sweets. Leeds produced many miniature creamware articles. These were not made (as is frequently thought) for travellers' samples—agents carried velvet-lined wooden boxes containing full-sized specimens to show as samples. The miniature pieces are consistently referred to in the potter's order books as toys.

One style of enamelling was painting in red monochrome; figures, landscapes, and flowers predominate. Also, there were articles with a bright, banded decoration, usually of rosy purple with little scattered flowers between stripes. Much of Leeds was shipped to Holland and decorated there, where the strong religious and patriotic feelings of the times were reflected in the painting. The Dutch palette consisted of brick red, a pale watery green, blue, maroon, black, flesh color, and yellow. The painting can be recognized by the mat quality of the colors.

Transfer printing was first used at Leeds soon after 1775. Leeds transfer printing is generally inferior to that of Sadler and Green at Liverpool. The colors used for the overglaze printing at Leeds were brick red, jet black, purplish black, and, after 1800, blue-black and gray. Prints of butterflies were often used for the lids of teapots and coffeepots.

Charming features of Leeds are the molded and decorative handles, spouts, and applied terminals at the extremities. The earliest were the crabstock handles and spouts and the strap handles with pinched ends. Other handles include the reeded double intertwined handle and twisted or rope handles with applied ter-

*Leeds creamware chestnut bowl
with perforated cover, c. 1790.*

minals at the ends. These terminals became an identifying feature of Leeds. The handles were also used by Wedgwood, although without the applied terminals.

Various knobs were attached to the lids, some in the shape of an acorn or mushroom, oval or round cauliflower, daisy, or strawberry. The Leeds flower knobs can easily be recognized, since they had a spray of two buds. The borders were gadrooned or feathered-edge, often used together in various colors.

In trying to produce a whiter paste and glaze, Wedgwood had discovered what is termed pearlware. The most important later production of Leeds was this pearlware, which was being made by 1790. The ware was coated with a glaze that sometimes ran into thick globules underneath or inside a piece, where it appears in a deep soft blue color, unlike that of the Staffordshire factories, where the blue is paler and has a slight tendency toward green. Leeds pearlware has a light bluish-gray color and possesses a richness and smoothness of surface that is extremely pleasing. The underglaze-blue painting effective on Leeds creamware was also used to decorate pearlware.

The first type of transfer-printed pearlware was in black overglaze. Leeds also excelled in printing a fine rich tint of underglaze blue. It did not produce many figures until the advent of pearlware, when charming figures were made, many of which are marked. These differ from the Staffordshire ones in that the plinth, or square base, upon which the figure stands has a greater depth.

Black stoneware produced by Leeds (called black basalt by Wedgwood and other Staffordshire potters) was, of the later productions, next in importance to pearlware. It was first made about 1800 and consisted, for the most part, of tea and coffee sets; there is no evidence that it extended to purely ornamental pieces. The details shown in the *Leeds Drawing Book for Black Ware* include lion, swan, and lapdog knobs. The most usual form of knob on Leeds blackware is the "widow with her barrel," of which variations were made by many other potters. Much of the basalt was stamped with the usual Leeds pottery impressed mark— LEEDS.

There is difficulty in identifying Leeds pottery by marks, since there is a scarcity of marked pieces. The finest examples of creamware were unmarked. The blue-printed ware after 1790 showed LEEDS-POTTERY (often printed twice over and crossing at right angles), HARTLEY, GREENS, & CO., LEEDS POTTERY (either in two lines or in a semicircle), and also the initials L.P.

To compound the difficulties, the creamware has appealed, because of its artistic qualities, to such a wide circle that it has often been forged. Unfortunately these pieces are marked "Leeds Pottery," L.P., or "Leeds P." The basket and similar designs have in recent years been made in Germany and sold to unwary buyers.

However, anyone who has had the opportunity of handling genuine old Leeds should not be taken in by these fraudulent pieces. Leeds ware is extremely light in weight, and the creamware varies in color from a pale, and sometimes very pale, cream color to a light buff. The peculiar color of the body, especially the slightly green tinge of the old Leeds creamware glaze, are not easily mistaken. The modern copies lack the fine potting, are heavier in weight, and have a thick, white, glossy glaze that fills the corners of the pierced work.

Leeds creamware coffeepot and a black basalt
rococo-shaped coffeepot, c. 1790.

Spode (1770 to present)

The name of Spode is almost as familiar to devotees of English ceramics as that of Wedgwood. Now known as the Spode Pottery at Stoke-on-Trent, it continues to operate under the name of Copeland or Copeland late Spode.

In the beginning, the Spode works manufactured only pottery, but by 1790 a porcelain body was introduced and added to the production. This phase of the factory's output is discussed in the chapter on bone china.

Josiah Spode was, like Josiah Wedgwood, apprenticed to Thomas Whieldon in 1749. By 1770, Spode had founded his own factory at Stoke-on-Trent in Staffordshire. He was a man of cultivation, intelligence, initiative, and sound business enterprise, all of which resulted in his building up a successful business. After his death, in 1797, his son, Josiah Spode II, continued to manage the company in the same tradition.

From 1770 Spode produced the usual contemporary wares—black basalt, stoneware jugs with hunting subjects (but smaller than similar ones made by Adams and Turner), and creamware.

Both Josiah Spode I and II experimented, and they made several innovations in the field of ceramics. The first of these was an improvement in transfer printing. Their early printing on creamware was in black over the glaze, but between 1781 and 1784, Josiah II began to use underglaze transfer-printed blue on creamware in different renditions of the Willow patterns introduced in 1780 by Turner at Caughley. By the beginning of the nineteenth century, Spode was producing about forty different designs in underglaze blue, on both cream and pearlware. Simeon Shaw stated in his

History of Staffordshire Pottery, published in 1829, "Josiah Spode II produced the best blue and white of his time." He had just cause to make such a statement. This underglaze-blue pearlware is always well potted, the glaze exceptional, and the printing of the pictures equally excellent. The borders do not run over the edges, and the joinings of patterns are difficult to perceive (in contrast to the wares of other potters); the pictures are very clear, and there is no smudging caused by carelessness in the transferring. In fact, the color of the blue in many cases approaches the best color of the Chinese K'ang-hsi porcelain.

The Spode underglaze blue that collectors most desire are the Indian Sporting and Caramanian (South Central Turkey) designs, because of their outstanding originality. The patterns for Indian Sporting were taken directly from the book *Oriental Field Sports with sketches by the author, Captain Thomas Williamson,* suitably worked up as aquatints for reproduction by Samuel Howitt, an artist well known for his drawings of animals. The Spode factory did not compete for the American trade as many Staffordshire potters were doing at this time; therefore none of the pottery carries American views.

Spode's answer to the blow that hit Georgian England's porcelain buyers in 1794 was "feldspar" porcelain. At this time importing porcelain from the Continent was prohibited, with the exception of Holland. Moreover, a duty of 30 percent was levied on all decorated porcelain whatever its origin. This raised the price of Oriental porcelains prohibitively, and china sellers were unwilling to renew their stocks of "Indian" porcelain. This resulted in a scarcity of dinner and dessert services, which were much in demand for important formal occasions.

Staffordshire potters took advantage of this situation by introducing substitutes for imported porcelain that would be hard, durable under the strain of dinner and table use, and suitable for lavish enamelling. Three potters patented a method of manufacturing "porcelain and earthenware"— Miles Mason, John Turner, and Josiah Spode II, all in 1800. Turner's venture ended in bankruptcy, and Mason and Spode became rich.

Spode's feldspar dinner and dessert services—hard, tough, white, translucent, and free from surface flaws—were welcomed by the china dealers. It was perfectly potted and could easily receive the gilding and rich, brilliant enamel colors in green, yellow, blue, olive, purple, rose, and brown —each in various tints—lavished upon it. Fashionable armorial services were produced, in which each piece displayed an expansive coat of arms in full color. The owners of small services of Chinese Export porcelain could add to them by ordering additional matching pieces in Spode's feldspar porcelain.

Spode continued to manufacture feldspar porcelain until the Copeland-Garrett partnership was formed in 1833, when production was abandoned. The mark, printed in puce, consisted of "Spode" in gothic letters above a wreath of rose, thistle, and shamrock, containing "Feldspar Porcelain" in script. This ware was intended to appeal to the professional man, the doctor, the lawyer, the wealthy merchant, and the well-to-do businessman who delighted in entertaining. These were Spode's chief customers for feldspar, not only in England but on the Continent and in America.

Josiah Spode II also introduced a less costly ceramic body that he named "stone china." The name stone china is misleading. It resembles hard porcelain only superficially and is not a porcelain in the usual sense. It is actually a good-quality glazed earthenware with a dense opaque body that makes a clear ring when lightly tapped. An improvement was made in stone china in 1810, and it was sold as "New Stone China."

"Killing Tiger," Spode Indian Sporting design,
in underglaze blue on pearlware, c. 1800.

Stone china was first painted by artists in enamel. Exact copies of East India patterns were produced, but soon adaptations more appealing to English tastes were made. An outstanding example is the peacock-and-peony pattern, in which a pair of peacocks face a large pink peony and a spray of prunus blossoms.

Spode's stone china rapidly established itself among the well-to-do, and its strength and attractive colors led to the fashion of huge dinner services, some with as many as 250 pieces. Spode marked his stone china with a square seal containing pseudo Chinese characters, the name SPODE across the middle, and STONE CHINA below. This was usually printed in blue.

All Spode made prior to 1800 was marked with impressed SPODE. The firm changed names on several occasions. Josiah Spode II died in 1827 and was succeeded by his son, Josiah, who only survived his father by two years. The business was continued by the executors and William Taylor Copeland until March 1, 1833, when Copeland purchased the concern. He took into partnership Thomas Garrett, and the Copeland and Garrett partnership continued from 1833 to the middle of 1847. At this time the partnership was dissolved, and William Copeland took his two sons into business with him.

Mason's Ironstone

With the ruling of 1794 prohibiting porcelain imports, Miles Mason, who was an importer of china, was faced with an exceedingly high sales loss. For this reason he established himself as a potter and by 1800 became sole proprietor of a pottery at Lane Delph, Staffordshire, where he specialized in the newly developed bone china. By 1804 he had evolved a stone china (similar to Spode's) that had a tough feldspathic earthenware glaze impervious to scratches, even those made by dinner knives. This stone china was decorated with enamels of exceptional brilliance and followed Spode's lead of Anglicizing versions of Oriental styles, although Mason's ware lacked the finer finish of Spode. Mason did excel in his blue-and-white imitation of Nanking. His business was so successful that by 1813 he retired as a very rich man, and the factory was transferred to his sons, George Mason (1789–1859) and Charles James Mason (1791–1856). In July 1813 Charles James Mason was granted a patent for a new ceramic body, exploited under the name of ironstone china, which was heavy in weight and opaque and possessed the great strength necessary for the monumental pieces that were being produced along with large dinner services, including punch bowls, bedposts, mantelpieces, and vases.

The predominant colors used on Mason's ironstone were mazarine blue, brick red, pink, and crimson, enamels that could be fired together. Much of this color was painted over black or blue transfer-printed lines. Ironstone china with its brilliant decoration (which continued largely in the "Japan" patterns), toughness, and comparative low cost proved to be extremely successful. Jugs were a Mason product that especially captured the imagination of the public. They were octagonal and plain in shape with snake handles.

George and Charles Mason produced immense quantities of ironstone china, but after their patent expired in 1827 many other potters began making it also, and their business was hurt by the competition. In the 1840s they changed their formula and added flint glass. This was termed "Improved Ironstone."

The earliest mark used on Mason was impressed MASON'S
PATENT IRONSTONE CHINA, followed around 1815 by a transfer-printed mark in red, puce, blue, or jet black. This was
made up of a crown with the name MASON'S above and
PATENT IRONSTONE CHINA in a cartouche below. There were
a number of variations in the details of the crown. In the
1840s, with the new body, the word PATENT was changed
to IMPROVED.

Other Staffordshire Potters

There were ten thousand master potters in Staffordshire in
the nineteenth century, and the majority produced wares
of quality. One of the outstanding characteristics of the
early nineteenth century (the Regency period) was the
high standard of craftsmanship. Practically all the ceramics
produced reveal originality of design and traits of the arti-
san's workmanship.

The names of many of these potters have faded into
oblivion because much of the ware was unmarked. There
are certain names that have become attached to similar
products of a maker although they bear no marks of identification. One of these is "Castleford." The output of David
Dunderdale's Castleford Potters can rightly be included
among Wedgwood's or Leeds' followers, since they engaged in the manufacture of black and red earthenware,
white and cane-colored stoneware, and cream-colored
earthenware. What is mainly associated with Castleford
are stoneware tea pieces that are translucent and actually
nearer to the later Parian ware than to true stoneware.
These are of a molded relief design, the ornaments in-
dented into the mold and not applied separately, as with
Wedgwood jasper relief. The designs are either hunting,
sporting, or rural in spirit. On the teapots, the neck and

upper part of the handle bear a brown or blue line. Some of the teapots were made with a sliding cover, and some had a hinged cover swinging on a metal pin.

Marked Castleford carries an impressed D.D. CASTLEFORD until 1803, followed by D.D. & C., CASTLEFORD, or D.D. & CO. CASTLEFORD POTTERY.

Many wares answering to the above description are falsely attributed to Castleford. Various potters from 1800 to 1825 made similar translucent stoneware. All of it, unless bearing the Castleford mark, should be regarded as Castleford type.

Another familiar name in Staffordshire pottery is "Wood," beginning during the second half of the eighteenth century with Ralph Wood I (1715–1772), who is probably the best-known and most-esteemed member of the family. His products consisted of figures covered in a colored lead glaze of yellow, green, brownish purple, or gray, applied in a manner that gives an effect of enamelling. These excel in quality and are highly collectible. A nephew of Ralph Wood I, Enoch Wood (1759–1840), was the most prolific member of the Wood family. For a time, he was a partner of Ralph Wood II, but in 1790 he entered into a partnership with James Caldwell that continued until 1818. He produced practically every type of ware, in the tradition of Wedgwood and followers, all of a high quality. Very few articles were marked, but when one was, it bore an impressed WOOD & CALDWELL. He specialized in figures. One of his best known is that of the Reverend John Wesley, modelled and signed "E. WOOD, Sculp. Burslem." This figure is eleven and a half inches tall and was probably made around 1785, before Wood went into partnership with Caldwell.

Enoch Wood was a talented modeller, and several fine plaques with a relief pattern bearing his signature or impressed mark are recorded. The word "Sculpsit" occurs after his name on several items that he modelled. Fine portrait busts, such as the one of John Wesley mentioned above, were also a feature of his work. The plaques are often in the style of Wedgwood, white reliefs on a blue jasper ground.

From 1818 to 1846 the firm was known as Enoch Wood & Sons; many pieces from this time are marked with an impressed or printed name or initials. During this period the factory produced fine patterned wares printed in underglaze cobalt blue for the American market. It has been stated that Enoch Wood & Sons was the largest exporter of earthenwares to America, and examples of his transfer-printed articles appear frequently in shops.

XV

Staffordshire Figures
and Historic Pottery

Staffordshire Figures

Staffordshire figures are endearing and appealing, not from
an artistic point of view but because they illustrate a way
of life in England. They were made in enormous quantities,
and the majority were unmarked. As the models were
imitated widely, it is difficult to know who was the first
modeller. They were not considered ceramic triumphs except in the few cases when they were proficiently modelled
and decorated with restrained coloring.

These little Staffordshire figures were at first known as
image toys, a term used by Josiah Wedgwood when record-

ing experimental work in 1752–1753. By the end of the century they were known merely as toys. In early nineteenth-century directories, makers of these figures were listed under the heading "Earthenware and China Toy Manufacturers." From 1820 potters referred to these figures as chimney ornaments.

The most familiar of the figures are the Victorian ones of countless subjects that were introduced about the time of the marriage of the young queen, Victoria, to Albert in 1840, a marriage that excited everyone's imagination.

The very valuable and scarce figures, seldom seen except in museums and in fine collections, are the ones from the so-called "early" and "best" periods, those made from about 1675 to 1760. The early period consisted, for the most part, of three-inch cats in stoneware or earthenware bodies with spots, or wavy lines and spots, of brown slip. Some of the cats were in three different colored clays, inter mingled and highly glazed; these were a bit taller, five to six inches.

The elder John Astbury is credited with a series of men, about six inches high, playing bagpipes or other musical instruments. These little men are splashed with brown and green and have yellow slip ornament. The lead glazing is warm and rich.

Surviving salt-glaze figures from this early period are very scarce and of exceptional interest.

Collectors regard the "Wood" school (*circa* 1760) as the "best" period for figures. The modelling of the elder Ralph Wood was strong and original; he was not in any way influenced by the classic revival in England at that time. He was a satiric potter, especially when it came to depicting the established church. There was a strong Quaker element in Staffordshire during this period, and "parson baiting" was a familiar form of amusement. Among his subjects were The Parson and Clerk Returning Home

After a Carousal, The Tithe Pig, and The Vicar and Moses, the latter showing the sleeping vicar, with full-bottomed wig, and Moses, the clerk, seated underneath the pulpit exhorting the congregation with uplifted hand. "The Vicar and Moses" has been copied by various potters, but in the copying they lose Wood's original strength and simplicity and also his restrained color. The imitations can be spotted by the brilliantly applied enamel colors.

William Pratt (1753–1799) was a master potter at Lane Delph who also may be placed in this period. The term "Pratt" is given to articles made at the end of the eighteenth century and in the early years of the nineteenth that are decorated with a distinctive palette of high-temperature colors, including a drab blue, yellow, ocher, dirty orange, dull green, and brown. Relief decorations are common. A few figures bear an impressed PRATT; all similar ware is termed "Pratt type." His son, Felix Pratt (1780–1859), continued the business. (See color insert, Pratt-type dishes.)

Pieces from the early 1800s become more homely. The potters began producing a number of mantel ornaments of a simple nature with rustic subjects suitable to a cottage home. The majority of these figures have no mark, and many were the productions of unrecorded potters working in a small way.

Among the names that are known is that of John Walton (1790–1839) of Burslem. He was a prolific maker of figures, using a cheap brittle earthenware capable of being produced at high speed for inexpensive markets such as fairs and village shops. He was the first Staffordshire potter to adapt the bocage of the mid-eighteenth-century porcelain makers to nineteenth-century pottery figures. He did this so well that the vogue spread to other potters. One such piece had a tree rising behind a figure or a group, which consisted of a short trunk supporting a few branches

*Early Staffordshire pottery figure
of a pug dog, c. 1760.*

thickly covered with conventional leaves carefully arranged by hand, each branch having in its center a colored flower. His well-known figure of a sheep with lamb is strongly modelled and coated with chippings from the turner's lathe to simulate wool. The lamb is placed below the sheep in a rocky recess of the green base. This model was made by other potters, but the wool was produced by mechanically tooling the surface of the ware. Some of these Walton figures had an impressed WALTON in a scroll on the back of the base. The title of the subject, such as "Lions" or "Lovers," was often inscribed on the front.

Ralph Salt of Hanley made large quantities of chimney ornaments from 1812 to 1846. His productions consisted of painted figures, especially bocage pieces, sporting dogs, and sheep with handmade wool. His mark was an impressed SALT either above or on a raised scroll. His son, Charles, a modeller who continued to operate the pottery until 1864, used as a mark an impressed SALT on the back of the plinth. His figures are not as well finished as his father's.

The plinth on these early nineteenth-century figures was usually square, shallow, and smooth on all surfaces. In the finer work the plinths were deeper. Groups often stood upon rocky bases, and the whole was usually supported by a plinth.

Since it was convenient to have a spill holder at hand near the fire to light your pipe, candle, or whatever, it was a popular chimney ornament. It generally consisted of a narrow vessel leaning against a supporting figure, man or beast.

Large cast figures were made from the 1830s, not only in Staffordshire but at the Scottish earthenware factories, Prestonpans Pottery and Rathbones Pottery at Portobello. These included full-length figures of celebrities, including Victoria and Albert, the royal family, Crimean and other

war heroes—such as Nelson, Wellington, Napoleon III—
the King of Sardinia, the Sultan of Turkey, and various
commanders in chief, contemporary sportsmen, and per-
sonalities of the stage, circus, and crime, as well as the
Scottish national heroes Wallace, Bruce, and Rob Roy.
The trade for which the potters aimed was not purely local,
so they made portraits of famous people of all countries.
America was well represented by Washington, Franklin,
Charlotte and Susan Cushman (actresses who went to
England in 1845 and played Romeo and Juliet), Mrs.
Amelia Bloomer (1818–1894), who introduced the popular
style of dress for women bearing her name, and characters
from Harriet Beecher Stowe's *Uncle Tom's Cabin*. These
large portrait figures were cast in simple plaster molds in
two parts. On the earlier ones there were large areas of
underglaze blue. Later a considerable amount of space was
left white.

Quantities of dogs were made, and they came to be regarded as a necessary ornament on the mantel shelf. The
dogs portrayed most often were the sporting dogs—grey-
hounds, foxhounds, Spanish pointers, usually all black or
all white, and setters. A popular figure was the dog referred to as a "comforter," a crossbreed of a Maltese and
the King Charles spaniel. Pottery "comforters" were made
in pairs, for "Her Lady's" drawing room or boudoir. Some
were as tall as eighteen inches and served as door porters.
The smallest were about six inches and were usually white
with colored ears and a few spots scattered over the body.
The nose is pink and the eyes have an almost human outline. A feature of the comforter is the small gold padlock
hanging from a collar around its neck and the little gold
chain across its chest that disappears over the back. There
were as many as two hundred patterns of this quaint
creature, which was finally outmoded by the Victorian

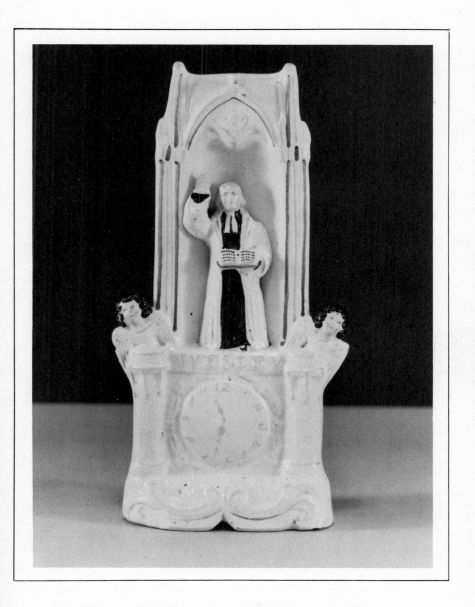

Staffordshire pottery figure of John Wesley, c. 1820.

pug. The spaniel and the clipped poodle were also extremely popular.

It is understandable that these earthenware dogs and figures have been vastly reproduced. Many of the reproductions are made from the old molds that are still in the hands of the Staffordshire potters. These are copied so perfectly that if it were not for the fact that the colors miss the correct period tints, they would be difficult to detect. The poorer copies are also modelled badly. Another fairly reliable test of authenticity is that the glaze is crazed on most old productions but not on present-day copies.

When buying Staffordshire figures, take into consideration that they were cottage ware produced in enormous quantities and are usually of inferior quality. Also, they have been reproduced in quantity for a number of years. I have in my possession a pair of spaniels that were given to me new in the 1920s. They are fifty years old and show wear on the base, but they are still reproductions. Often it is impossible to ascertain the correct age. Keep these facts in mind when searching for Victorian figures. Do not be so carried away by their charm that you disregard the high price that frequently is asked. The authentic wares of the "early" or "best" periods, on the other hand, are highly collectible objects and in great demand. When available, these rightly bring very high prices, often in three figures.

Transfer-Printed Historic Wares

Transfer printing of designs on porcelain and pottery was discovered in mid-eighteenth-century England. This discovery, one of the few entirely British contributions to the potter's art, revolutionized the ceramic industry. Prior to this invention ceramics, when decorated, were either painted under the glaze or in enamel colors over the glaze, all by hand. The new method made it possible to produce cheaper wares and in larger quantities.

There have been various claims as to who was the first to use transfer printing. John Brooks, an Irish engraver, while living in Birmingham applied for a patent for printing on enamel and china dated September 10, 1751. He was registered as a partner in the firm of Janssen, Delamain & Brooks at York House, Battersea, London, in 1753, which closed in 1756. There are Battersea enamels with transfer-printed decoration from the year 1753–54. It is also known that Robert Hancock, working at the Worcester porcelain factory, used transfer designs around 1756. Now, however, it is generally conceded that the credit for the new process of transfer printing on porcelain and pottery belongs to John Sadler of Liverpool. The following quote is taken from the *Liverpool Guide*, published in 1790: "Copper plate printing upon china and earthenware originated here in 1752, and remained some time a secret with the inventors, Messrs. Sadler and Green."

Shortly after 1748, Sadler became associated in business with Guy Green of New Market, Liverpool, and together they operated their "Printed Ware Manufactory" under the trade name "Sadler and Green." As a result of seven years of experimenting to find a more facile form of decorating pottery, they were able to print twelve hundred tiles of different patterns in six hours (recorded on July 27, 1756). John Sadler made a fortune with his new process and retired from the business about 1770. Guy Green continued alone until 1799.

Sadler and Green decorated cream-colored earthenware for Liverpool and Staffordshire potters. In enamel colors, mainly black but also brick red and a little later various shades of brown and purple, the design was applied over the glaze and refired in an enamel kiln at a low temperature to set the color.

As outlined previously, the process was as follows: A design was etched onto a piece of copper, and while the copper was still hot, the ceramic color was rubbed into it. A spatula was used to remove the excess paint and make it smooth, and then the copper was carefully wiped with a soft cloth. Wet tissue was then placed on the hot copper, and the whole was put between rollers. The tissue, having received a reverse print of the ceramic color, was then peeled off and pressed with a sticky substance onto the object to receive the design. This process was repeated on each article to be so decorated.

Plates, dishes, teapots, platters, and other articles in cream-colored earthenware were done in this manner, but the major output was pitchers, bowls, and mugs. The early transfer designs depicted flowers, pastoral scenes, classical figures, and homely English peasant groups. After the American Revolution and the signing of the Treaty of Paris, in 1783, the English potters, being trade-minded, made every effort to obtain their share of the growing American market, and Liverpool pottery was decorated for the American trade by using transfer designs of American interest. These included portraits of American heroes who had been prominent in the struggle for independence; portraits of presidents; allegories of liberty, commerce, peace, and plenty; Masonic emblems; naval engagements; and stock pictures of merchant ships, which appear and reappear, bearing different names and flags. These latter were made mainly to attract the American shipmasters calling at the port of Liverpool.

Anglo-American transfer-decorated creamware was made also at other English potteries. Little effort has been made to distinguish between earthenware made in the Liverpool district and that made in factories in other parts of England, since paste and glaze are very similar and the application of the transfer print was made on individual pieces of different kinds and sizes according to the whim of the potter or the fancy of the purchaser. The name assigned to the subject portrayed on the article is an unreliable clue, and since the ware is seldom signed, it offers no information as to where it was made or the date of manufacture. For these reasons it is all given the generic term "Liverpool."

Creamware with transfer-printed designs of American interest is eagerly sought. In the past it was often found in New England seaport towns in the possession of descendants of sea captains and sailors who had brought it back as presents from England. Little has survived, and naturally the scarcity has caused a great increase in value, but since these wares portray a picture of America's past in an inimitable manner, in spite of their high price they should be seriously considered for collecting. Their value will continue to increase.

After the breakthrough of transfer printing, potters continued to experiment, hoping to expand the use of this process further. They were anxious to discover how to print successfully under the glaze on earthenware. Although the overglaze transfer print was clearer in detail, it lacked the protection of the glaze and for that reason was less durable. Underglaze printing would have the added advantage of requiring one less firing.

It was known that the only color to survive the high temperature of the glost oven was a blue pigment derived from cobalt oxide. This had been used on the underglaze painted wares of China. Underglaze blue printing was introduced on soft paste at Worcester by 1760 and used sucessfully at Bow and Lowestoft soon after. From the 1780s the Caughley works used it to an even greater extent. It was at Caughley that underglaze-blue printing was first used on pottery, the first pattern being the well-known Willow.

Although underglaze-blue transfer printing on pottery originated in Shropshire, it was soon taken up by the Staffordshire potteries, and all earthenware with underglaze printing is generally termed "Staffordshire." This cheaper method of decoration spread rapidly to the large factories and was also soon adopted by the many smaller potteries; in time, it became almost universal. As it grew in fashion, cream-colored wares with overglaze painting or printing lessened in demand.

By 1810, blue-printed earthenware was being produced in large quantities. Peak production was between 1820 and 1840, when blue-printed earthenware was exported all over the world. Up until about 1830 blue was, with few exceptions, the only color used on the Staffordshire. It was cheap and went on easily, and its density covered imperfections in the ware and workmanship, such as blisters in the glaze and marks of the triangles used to separate the articles in the kiln. Around 1830, the rich deep blue was followed with paler tints—light blue, green, mulberry, purple, gray, and also black. By mid-Victorian times it had descended to what is referred to as "flow" or "flown" blue. By 1835, more green- and pink-printed underglaze pottery was being exported to America than the blue-printed wares.

The subjects of the engravings used for decoration were extremely diverse. The early patterns were designs derived from the Chinese, combined with geometric borders. As time went on, novelty of design became a primary concern. No subject escaped the potters' attention: romantic pastoral landscapes; the fashionable Grand Tour of the Continent; views in Asia Minor, Egypt, Palestine, and the Ottoman Empire; views English water colorists had painted on their journeys in the British Isles; abbeys, castles, cathedrals, colleges, and other places of interest. Not only scenic views were used but also amusing subjects inspired by the work of caricaturists and illustrators. James Clews produced the Doc-

tor Syntax designs after the originals by the English carica-
turist T. Rowlandson, and the Wilkie Series from the
scenes of lowly country life by the artist Sir David Wilkie.

Around 1802 geometric borders began being replaced by
the strip borders in vogue on wallpapers. These borders
were composed of flower and foliage festoons, fruiting vines,
sea shells, and floreate scrolls interspersed with bellflowers
or butterflies. Many potters adopted special borders. A potter
might pirate another's popular view, but rarely did he steal
another's border. The morning glory is associated with
Thomas Godwin, the eagle border with Joseph Stubbs, and
the shell border with Enoch Wood. It is often possible to
identify the maker by the border, although there are many
unidentified borders and potters.

The most valuable Staffordshire in the United States are
the articles that carry designs portraying life in America.
The potters who had gained the American trade after 1783
lost it with the War of 1812. Many were eager to regain
their foothold and put aside allegiance to their own country
to appeal to the nationalism of the young United States.
Staffordshire potters flooded this country with attractive inexpensive pottery for household use. The ware had designs
of the early history of the country, portraits of military and
political leaders, the new cities, public buildings, historic
sights, mountains, rivers, lakes, oceans, public transport, and
perhaps the most important, the daily lives of our fore-
fathers, their homes, dress, neighborhoods, modes of travel,
even their ideology. Generally the scenes were accurate, since
many of the views were taken from the sketches of Bartlett
and Cole and other artists of the time. The United States in
1820 was proud of its short history, and people were attracted by these portrayals of their country. The owners displayed this pottery with great pride, just as present-day
collectors do.

From about 1890 through the first two decades of the

twentieth century there was a great urge to find and collect this historic Staffordshire, and it was purchased at very high prices, collectors vying with each other to get a particular plate or coffeepot. There were magazine articles on the subject in the 1890s and several books in the early 1900s. Some of the bigger collections were made at this time, accompanied by complete records of where it was found, what it cost, and so on. This was followed by the usual fluctuation of interest and prices went down for a number of years, but now, again, when it comes up at auction or on the market, it brings the high prices it rightfully deserves.

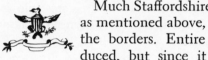 Much Staffordshire pottery is unmarked, but, as mentioned above, some can be identified by the borders. Entire table services were produced, but since it was used extensively as "everyday china," not too much has survived. Articles decorated with American subjects in the brilliant deep dark blue are the rarest and costliest. There are beautifully potted pieces with English and picturesque scenes in dark blue as well as in a medium-dark blue that is highly regarded. Potters who produced this ware were the different members of the Adams family, Ralph and James Clews, Davenport, Ralph Hall, Joseph Stubbs, T. Mayer, Ridgway, Enoch Wood, and Andrew Stevenson, among many others both known and unknown.

With the more common subjects, care should be given to buying objects in good condition, but it is well to buy even damaged pottery with American subjects if it is reasonably priced.

Toby Jugs and Lusterware

It is with reluctance that the subject of toby jugs and lusterware is introduced into this book. Both are familiar

*"Lafayette at Washington's Tomb," underglaze-blue
Historic Staffordshire pottery,
unidentified border and maker, c. 1820.*

to most beginners and are in demand to some degree. They are reproduced in great quantities, and the reproductions are sold without any intention of deception in practically every gift shop. It is impossible for the beginner to distinguish between the newly made tobies and lusterware and the old. Copies are found in antique or junk stores and also appear in garage or house sales. The unwary buyer is often taken in.

The toby jug was designed for convivial pleasure. It is said to have been named for a thirsty old soul, Toby Philpot, whose habit was not temperance. He is usually depicted with both hands occupied, either holding mug and jug, or a pipe, and he often has an expression delightful in its benevolence. There are also some with disagreeable and leering faces, quite enough to dispel all wish for any libation they contain. Often the brim of the three-cornered hat forms the lip of the jug, and the crown is a detachable cover or cup.

These were made in earthenware by Ralph Wood, James Neale, Lakin and Poole, Spode, Davenport, and others in Staffordshire, Yorkshire, and other areas. There were altogether about thirty varieties, including such subjects as The Gin Woman, The Snuff Taker, John Bull, Pickwick, The Thin Man, The Night Watchman, The Sailor, and Punch.

Some well-modelled copies of toby jugs were produced about fifty years ago and are very difficult to distinguish from the original ones. A particularly good one, with a salt-glaze surface, has Toby seated in a corner chair; another "fake" has a Whieldon-style mottled base and hat. Some of these copies can be spotted because of their blatant coloring, smudged and smeared with black stains to simulate age.

Toby jugs are quaint and amusing, but collecting them seriously should be approached with caution. It is one thing to acquire them for ornament and another for a collection. Before paying the price asked for good specimens, serious study should be made, so that a copy can be distinguished from an original old toby.

Much the same can be said about collecting lusterware. Often a new article of luster can be detected, since there will be no signs of wear on the bottom, whereas some of the luster is worn off of the old pieces from use over the years. Also, with the new pieces the shades of color are brighter and they have a glassy glare, rather than the depth and richness of the old.

Luster is usually on an earthenware body. It may be divided into the following classes:

GOLD LUSTER, probably invented by Josiah Wedgwood II c. 1805. This is not to be confused with gilding. The effect varies from pink to purple.

PLATINUM OR SILVER LUSTER, discovered by Thomas Wedgwood, used for imitations of silverware and busts.

COPPER OR BRONZE LUSTER, plain and undecorated.

GOLD OR PURPLE LUSTER used as an adjunct or slight decoration, either as a band or a rim.

PLATINUM OR SILVER LUSTER used as an adjunct or slight decoration.

PLATINUM OR SILVER LUSTER used in combination with other painted decorations, such as birds or foliage, which are painted in silver luster on a ground of another color, or in silver luster "resist" (described in Chapter IV), when the ground is platinum and the ornamentation is white, blue, or yellow. This technique dates from 1810.

COPPER OR BRONZE LUSTER in combination with painted design.

The majority of lusterware is unmarked. Pieces of silver luster have been found with the name of "Wood and Caldwell" impressed on them, which was that firm's mark from 1790 to 1818. Another name found impressed on plain silver lusterware of early-Georgian shape is "E. Mayer." Among other makers known to have produced silver luster are Robert Wilson of Hanley, his brother David Wilson,

Lakin and Poole, Spode, and Davenport. Swansea is credited with gold and gold-purple luster on a marbled ground.

Copper or bronze luster is thought to have been introduced later than silver luster. This bronze or copper luster varies considerably. It may be coarse brown ordinary ware, or it may be very thin and delicate. The best copper or bronze luster has painted views in panels against the lustrous background. Very often copper luster jugs and mugs have ornamentation in relief that is enamelled in vivid colors. This has been reproduced widely and poorly.

The luster jugs came in all sizes, from miniature ones to large ones used in taverns. Mugs, cups, vases, and various small articles are found with luster decoration. New Hall produced deep dishes and cups and saucers in bone china edged and lined in pink luster with black transfer-printed scenes in cavetto. Many of these depict memorials to Princess Charlotte.

About 1840 a less expensive range of luster made from copper oxide was issued, and after 1845 the quality of luster began to decline. This new ware, liable to be disfigured with specks, pinholes, pimples, and bubbles, is distinctly heavier than the earlier ware.

Prices vary dependent on the quality of the ware. It must be reiterated that discretion must be observed when purchasing either toby jugs or lusterware.

XVI

Bone China and Nineteenth-Century Porcelains

The nineteenth century saw many innovations in English ceramics after the importation of porcelain was prohibited in 1794. The soft paste ware made in the eighteenth century was unsuitable for dinner services because the paste and glaze could not stand up under the wear of the cutlery. The china sellers who had depended on the Continental hard paste porcelain to supply their customers with dinnerware were now unable to replace their stocks.

Josiah Spode responded to this situation with a new porcelain body. He evolved a china of uniform translucence, and eliminated frit by adding calcined bones to the body, which were distributed with heavier components. This porcelain proved to be the nearest to Oriental porcelain yet devised for practical use in England. Spode had experimented with Cornish china clay and Cornish china stone, although Cookworthy and later Champion had been granted a monopoly forbidding its use for translucent ware by any other factory. Spode was allowed these ingredients for his opaque ware and therefore had access to them for experiments. The consequence was the discovery of bone china, which became the standard English china in the nineteenth century.

Although methods of preparation and firing caused vast improvements in the body, the formula remained the same —six parts bone ash, four parts Cornish stone, and three and a half parts Cornish clay. The bone ash is responsible for the milky-white translucence and also tended to prevent crazing of the biscuit in the event of overfiring.

It had a high tendency to shrink, and care was required in drying and firing to prevent distortion and fire cracks. The glaze was a transparent glass made of silica, lead oxide, and potash, sufficiently fusible for overglaze enamels to sink into and adhere to without subsequent flaking.

A large amount of the early bone china was flawed. It had minute black specks, particularly the ware made by the small potters. On the costly pieces these specks were covered with colored opaque enamels, ground colors, and gilding.

Spode's account books record that a limited quantity of bone china was marketed in 1794; by 1796 trade had increased to such an extent that he had to acquire a larger warehouse in London to accommodate additional demand.

Until July 1796, no other potters were producing bone china, but soon after, Spode was joined by Duesbury and Kean, Derby; Thomas Minton, Stoke-on-Trent; John Rose, Coalport; Chamberlain & Co., Worcester; Worthington, Humble and Holland, Liverpool; and John Davenport,

Longport. By 1812 the Wedgwood Company, New Hall, and many others were producing it.

One very highly regarded producer of bone china was the Rockingham factory, on the Swinton estate of Earl Fitzwilliam. It produced exceptional-quality bone china from 1820 until 1841. There were also at least eighteen lesser-known Staffordshire potters producing bone china by 1818, much of which is unmarked. This unmarked china from the lesser firms is often, and without reason, classed as "Rockingham," and rides falsely on that factory's fine reputation.

It is often very difficult to attribute unmarked bone china to a particular firm. The paste used at all the factories was standard mixture and often handled in the same way. Workers and decorators moved from factory to factory. Quantities of bone china were decorated by independent enamellers working for china sellers who bought from various potters in the white. Their customers then selected patterns from folios of hand-painted designs and sample ware. In these cases, it is impossible to identify the factory from the decoration. Occasionally identification can be made by the ground colors used, since tints varied with individual potters. Such firms as Minton, Copeland, Rose of Coalport, and several unknown independent decorators, for instance, produced ground colors of exceptional beauty. (See color insert, English bone china plate.)

Only the most notable bone china manufacturers and their type of output will be described here. Unmarked bone china without any distinguishing qualities for attribution should be judged by the quality of the ware, decoration, and condition. Age can usually be determined by the contour or shape. All bone china is nineteenth- or twentieth-century, but the period it was made in may be determined by whether the shape is more classic, Greek Revival, or Victorian (see pp. 24–5).

Spode

Since Josiah Spode was the first to introduce bone china,
and the factory under the name of "Copeland late Spode"
continues to make bone china to the present day, there is
probably more Spode available than any other bone china.
The body of the ware is a paste of rich tone, white and
translucent, without being glassy. The glaze is clear and
transparent and not cold and glittering like the glazes on
some of the hard paste Continental ware. The Spode
pattern books and ledgers of the 1820s indicate the wide
variety of ware made at that time. There are artichoke cups,
asparagus trays, broth bowls, butter tubs and stands, card
racks, chamber candlesticks with extinguishers, cheese
dishes, cheese toasters, chestnut vases, chicken tureens, cus-
tard cups, cylinder screw-top pin cases, ice pails, inkstands
and pen trays, match pots, mugs, radish trays, roll trays, root
dishes, rouge pots, salad bowls, sandwich sets, scent jars,
snuffboxes, snuffer trays, steak dishes with compartments,
strawberry baskets, sugar boxes, supper plates, syrup pots,
toast racks, turtle pans, violet baskets, and wafer boxes.
Punch and toddy bowls ranging from two-gallon to quart
capacity were decorated in matching sets.

With entertainment in the home on such a grand scale,
and with the frequent large-sized households, enormous
dinner, dessert, and tea services were produced. These are
elaborately enamelled and gilded, and in many cases followed the fashion of painting each piece with the family
coat of arms in full color. Often the coats of arms are not
genuine.

One of the more distinctive types of decoration employed in the early days of the Spode factory was what is

sometimes known as the "Crown Derby Japan Pattern," although the Spode pattern books show this long before the flood of Japanese designs from the Derby factory. The Spode patterns, with deep velvety blues and rich gold, were derived from the Japanese Imari porcelain. Josiah Spode II was an accomplished designer whose leanings toward the Oriental led to the production of an excessive amount of china with Chinese designs, although both English and French types of design were represented, and the Spode Oriental patterns often carry a strong English flavor.

Decorations on Spode include floral subjects, fruits, birds, landscapes, and figures, all with rich gilding. They were used both with and without ground colors. Transfer-printed outlines were applied and color was filled in with a brush.

The more frequently used ground colors are dark blue, scale blue, apple green, yellow, gray, marbled brown, turquoise, striped red and gold, crimson, marbled blue, salmon, green, lavender, canary and blue, solid gold, and dotted or stippled gold, as well as gold scale on a blue ground.

The marks on Spode china are plainly displayed and show the various changes in the directors of the firm at different dates.

Minton China (1798 to present)

Up until 1798 Minton produced only white earthenware ornamented in blue in imitation of Nanking. In 1799 the factory produced a semitransparent china, but since it was not successful it was abandoned in 1811 and not resumed until 1821. By this time the experimental days of bone china were over, and Minton followed the best traditions of the day in making and decorating it. The decoration was always good, and the articles are plainly marked, so it is easy to identify. Minton produced a white body, seldom flawed; therefore it could be lightly decorated. The glaze is lustrous and the enamelling brilliant. From the early 1830s, Minton's ground colors display exceptionally beautiful tints. They were based on various combinations of pure gold with salts of ammonia and other chemicals. From these emerged the splendid carmine purple, Sèvres green, turquoise blue, rose du Barry, and Vincennes blue of the late 1840s. The Minton firm has been described as "a veritable branch of the Sèvres manufactory in matters of taste."

Most of Minton is marked so it is easy to identify. The early marks were MINTON or M impressed; from 1831 MINTON & BOYLE was impressed and a blue-printed mark, composed of an elaborate cartouche enclosing the pattern name and the initials M & B, was used. After 1841, MINTON & CO. was impressed. During this period, too, a blue enamelled mark resembling the crossed L's of Sèvres with the initial M was in use on fine porcelain and cabinet ware. The pattern number may be painted below. The globe with the name MINTON inscribed across the equator was used in variations from 1868 until the end of the century. Use of the name MINTONS dates from the late 1870s. Date-of-manufacture symbols were printed or impressed from 1842. These serve as an accurate way to date an article.

Wedgwood Bone China
(1812–1822, 1878 to present)

The Wedgwood factory was slow in entering the field of bone china. Under Josiah Wedgwood I, the firm had introduced and perfected many fine earthenwares, mainly Queen's Ware, jasper, basalt, terra-cotta, and caneware. Josiah Wedgwood II did not possess the business acumen or experimental nature of his father, and when his father died in 1795, he just continued producing the same still-fashionable, high-quality earthenwares. Finally, with the urging and encouragement of his partner and head of the London business, Thomas Byerley, he began making bone china in 1812.

When Wedgwood's bone china was first placed on the market, it was unsuccessful. However, the following season proved to be better, since a large variety of patterns were in demand by the gay Regency society. The china is called "Wedgwood's Regency Ware," and the patterns that decorate it reflect the garish taste of that era.

The pattern range was considerable. The first important order was for a blue-printed Chinese landscape pattern of the Willow type. It was followed by another Oriental-influenced pattern, described as "Chinese flowers in red brown and colors, with gold edge." This latter pattern proved popular, and several colors were used. Floral motifs, taken mostly from *Pillement's Flowers*, were popular; complying with the taste of the times, the decorative treatment was brighter than Wedgwood usually produced. These botanical designs were printed and enamelled over and lack fine detail.

The range of wares produced in bone china includes tea, coffee, and fruit services, and smaller decorative items, such as inkwells, miniature baskets, and some small vases. Many of the Regency shapes used were new ones for the Wedgwood factory, since they had continued in the classical manner.

The quality of Wedgwood bone china is extremely uneven, some of it being closer to a pearlware body and very dense. This was in contrast to the quality of their earthenware, which surpassed their contemporaries. Other examples, mostly small decorative items, are of the finest quality, and often superior to the best productions of the traditional bone china being produced at other factories during this period.

Orders have been found for Wedgwood's bone china up until 1822. However, during the few years preceding that there was a falling off of demand. In 1820 Wedgwood began to manufacture stone china, a much denser and cruder ware. This and the "New Pearl Ware" resulted in the termination of bone china production. Only in the last few years have admirers of Wedgwood turned their attention to its bone china. The rarity of the ware will make it increasingly valuable.

The manufacture of porcelain was revived at Wedgwood, Etruria, in 1878 and continues to the present day.

Wedgwood bone china from the 1812–1822 period is always marked. WEDGWOOD is printed either in red or blue or sometimes in gold in upper-case letters, over the glaze, a fact which often results in the partial obliteration of the mark. When the manufacture of bone china was resumed in 1878, a duplicate of the Portland vase with WEDGWOOD underneath was printed in black and other colors. In 1891, in compliance with the new American customs regulations, the word "England" was added to WEDGWOOD.

Davenport Bone China (c. 1820–1822)

The factory founded in 1792 by John Davenport at Longport, a suburb of Burslem, for the manufacture of blue-printed earthenware produced every kind of earthenware and porcelain prolifically until 1882. Davenport achieved outstanding success from the very beginning with his openwork rimmed dishes and plates. Around 1800 he began making good-quality stone china and by 1820 was producing a bone china. This first bone china had a slightly grayish tone, but it was soon improved so that the body, glaze, and workmanship of Davenport china are of the highest order.

Like Spode and Derby, Davenport adapted the popular Oriental patterns to the English taste—so skillfully, in fact, that a casual observer might mistake Davenport stone china for Oriental hard paste porcelain. Flower and fruit decorations were enamelled in naturalistic colors. Gold was used profusely; handles, feet, rims, and borders were heavily gilded and brilliantly burnished. Borders of encrusted flowers enclose painted landscapes on ornamental and cabinet ware. Major use was made of ground colors, particularly apple green, gray, and orange. Elaborate dinner, dessert, tea, and coffee services and vases were extensively produced.

The popularity of Davenport's china is derived from the excellence of its body and its exquisite designs and embellishments. King William IV, coming to the throne in 1830, ordered a superb service of Davenport porcelain for his coronation banquet. The whole was modelled in an original fashion from carefully chosen drawings. The larger pieces had sculptures from models furnished by some of the finest artists in the kingdom. His Majesty testified in the warmest manner to his gratification in finding in his own country a factory capable of producing such a display of art, which "could scarcely be equalled, not to say surpassed, by any other." Royalty continued to patronize the factory. Queen Victoria used a Davenport service at the Civic Banquet in 1837.

John Davenport retired in 1831, at age sixty-five, owning several other factories in Longport and employing about fifteen hundred workmen. There were branches in London, Liverpool, Hamburg, and Lübeck. The business was continued by his sons, Henry and William Davenport, who continued to enlarge and add factory buildings until about 1882.

Notwithstanding the fact that an abundance of articles is available from this long-operated prolific factory, the price tag is usually high, especially on the marked pieces of bone china made during the first decade of production.

Not all the output is marked. Some of the marks used are the name DAVENPORT impressed in the clay and also painted or printed; DAVENPORT LONGPORT and DAVENPORT LONGPORT STAFFORDSHIRE; and an anchor with the word DAVENPORT impressed or stamped in color.

Rockingham Bone China (1820–1842)

The name "Rockingham" calls to mind a porcelain of the highest quality, profusely decorated with well-executed painting, colored grounds, and lavish gilt, usually molded in rococo shape. This pottery at Swinton in Yorkshire was established around 1745 and at that time made a brown stoneware. Later a close association with Leeds resulted in its wares bearing a resemblance to Leeds productions. The factory developed a rich manganese-brown glaze that became known as the "Rockingham glaze." Also associated with it is the "Cadogan teapot," derived from a Chinese winepot of peach shape that, lacking an opening at the top, was filled through the bottom.

Rockingham, which had come into the possession of four brothers—Thomas, George, Frederick, and John Wagner Brameld—began making bone china about 1820. Their ambition was to produce the most luxurious porcelain in the world, and with that in mind they selected the finest material in England, attracted the most experienced craftsmen from Staffordshire and Derby, and employed the most advanced potting technique. The bone china products were so costly that the factory could not absorb the financial strain. The brothers obtained aid from Charles, Marquis of

Rockingham (Earl Fitzwilliam), on whose estate they were operating. At this time, 1826, the business was renamed Rockingham Works, and the Fitzwilliam crest of a griffin passant was introduced as the factory trademark.

In every respect of paste, glaze, decoration, gilding, and modelling, Rockingham excelled. During the 1830s the wares surpassed the majority of the competition and embodied the most florid taste of the rococo period. The ground colors include a thick opaque apple green peculiar to Rockingham and blue in several tints, among which were a *gros bleu* verging on violet, a soft mazarine, and sky blue. The red grounds ranged from deep pink to a maroon, similar to Chelsea's; the yellow was darker than the yellow used at Derby. Delicate peach was occasionally used and is very rare. A favorite decoration was a pink ground gilded in diaper patterns. Ground colors were also gilded with a lacelike pattern. Often gilding was applied lavishly, and large areas of gold were used for wide borders, handles, and knobs. This gold was burnished brilliantly. The Rockingham gold often has a faintly coppery tinge acquired through long exposure, but this work is usually marked and not to be confused with lesser-quality ware attributed to Rockingham.

Compotes, dishes, and plates often have molded edges in relief, which radiate with gilded scrollwork, and there are gilded veins to the leaf-shaped handles. Patterns with naturalistic flowers and lifelike butterflies and insects in full color against a yellow ground were particularly popular, and there are tea cups with interiors painted with views and the exterior richly gilded. Among the unusual modelled ware are flower-encrusted articles, baskets woven from straw of bone china and painted white, off-white, or cane, and pot-pourri bowls massed with tiny flowers. Wall plaques were painted with the familar garden flowers—tulips, dahlias, primulas, and roses—against a highly glazed white ground.

During the third decade of the nineteenth century this factory revived rococo styles with rare distinction. Familiarity with this superb porcelain should bring an end to the practice of ascribing unmarked wares of inferior quality of this period to Rockingham, but meanwhile caution should be taken in purchasing "Rockingham." The values of true Rockingham far exceed similar wares from less-experienced potters.

Rockingham bone china made before 1826 was seldom marked. An oval medallion impressed with the name "Brameld" encircled with a wreath of national emblems was sometimes applied to better-quality ware. The name BRAMELD is occasionally impressed or printed in red or purple. With Earl Fitzwilliam's backing in 1820, the firm began to use printed marks. First came a griffin passant above the copperplate inscription ROCKINGHAM WORKS, BRAMELD. This may be in red, purple, or brown. In 1830 the griffin was surmounted by the royal crown with the inscription MANUFACTURE TO THE KING below the factory name. After 1837 the word KING was altered to QUEEN. By 1840 marks containing royal references were no longer permissible, and the mark reverted to the griffin used between 1829 and 1830.

Ridgway Bone China (c. 1813–1858)

The name Ridgway is associated with several factories that prior to producing bone china were making good earthenware. Job Ridgway (1759–1814) built Cauldon Place Works, Hanley, in 1802 and operated it with his sons, John and William, under the name Ridgway and Sons. The porcelain produced was of admirable quality and some of it displayed decoration that was rich, elaborate, and well executed, including such subjects as flowers, fruit, birds, landscapes, and figures. The favorite ground colors were deep blue, green, and rose Pompadour. The gilding was rich and excellently applied.

After Job died in 1814, the sons carried on under the name J. & W. Ridgway until 1830, when William established the Bell Bank Pottery and absorbed at least six other firms, including Elijah Mayer and Son; Hicks, Meigh & Johnson; and Palmer & Wilson. He traded as W. Ridgway & Co. John continued the Cauldon Place Works with the aid of partners under the trademark of John Ridgway & Co. This factory received the distinction of becoming the Queen's potter in 1842, and in 1851 the Jury of the Great Exhibition rated him as one of the most important potters in the country. The firm was sold in 1855.

The wares made by John continued in the same fine tradition as when his father was alive. He produced almost every type of ware in bone china and earthenware, from inexpensive to costly tableware. Cabinet pieces are rare. Translucent cane-colored ware was popular, and a product distinct to this factory.

Up until 1814 the pottery when marked bore an impressed "J. Ridgway" and RIDGWAY & SONS. Printed marks include J. RIDGWAY over a potter's kiln until 1814; a shield containing the pattern name and the initials JWR in script until 1830; JOHN RIDGWAY & CO. / CAULDON PLACE / POTTERS TO HER MAJESTY, with the royal arms above and BY ROYAL APPOINTMENT below from 1842.

Coalport Bone China (c. 1796 to present)

Although Coalport has been previously discussed (Chapter XII), it deserves to be included here along with other prominent factories producing bone china because of the excellent grade of work accomplished under John Rose II and later by his nephew, William Rose. They raised Coalport decoration to a high level.

John Rose II was awarded the Gold Medal of the Royal Society of Arts for one of his ceramic achievements, the introduction of a leadless, feldspathic glaze. Because the lead had been poisoning factory workers in the pottery industry, the Society of Arts had offered a premium "to the person who shall discover the cheapest, safest, most durable, and most fusible composition fit for the purposes of glazing earthenware, without any preparation of lead, arsenic, or other pernicious ingredients, and superior to any hitherto in use."

On dinner services and ornamental wares Coalport used a variety of ground colors, many in imitation of Sèvres. Turquoise was especially popular. Also found is the deep mazarine blue that was famous at Derby, pink, claret, a bright canary yellow, and gray. The articles were frequently gilded and accompanied with molded relief work enriched with gilding. A wide variety of decorations were employed, including all manner of floral subjects, garlands, festoons, wreaths, landscapes, figures, gaily feathered birds, and heraldic devices in the reserved panels, either with or without ground colors.

In 1820 Rose purchased both the Swansea and Nantgarw factories, and William Billingsley and Samuel Walker, the proprietors, were engaged by Rose. For a period from about 1820 to 1830, Rose used a porcelain formula very similar to that of Nantgarw, causing the Coalport porcelain to be remarkably translucent. Billingsley continued to paint his well-known roses and other exquisite flowers, adding to the charm of Coalport.

From about 1850 there was a revived fashion for the Japan patterns that had been so freely used during the early years of the factory. The craftsmanship of the later Japan patterns can be distinguished from the earlier work by the extreme precision and regularity. Colors, especially the deep reds and a blue with a purplish cast, were fuller than formerly.

There was a slump in the production of fine china at Coalport from about 1860 to 1880, when there was a renewed interest. Old designs were revived with all the old beauty and grace, and new designs and patterns were introduced. Originality was encouraged, resulting in high achievement.

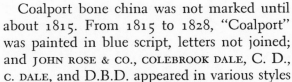 Coalport bone china was not marked until about 1815. From 1815 to 1828, "Coalport" was painted in blue script, letters not joined; and JOHN ROSE & CO., COLEBROOK DALE, C. D., c. DALE, and D.B.D. appeared in various styles of script. The blue or gold monogram C.B. D was used from the late 1840s to the early 1860s. This was succeeded until 1875 by a C combined with an S scroll forming three loops containing the letters C.SN in gold, occasionally in red or blue. The mark COALPORT AD 1750 was used on biscuit taken from stock after 1865 and on productions between 1875 and 1881. The misleading date is that of the pottery's beginning—Caughley was started that year and acquired later by Coalport. From 1881 until 1892 this mark was used with the addition of a crown. The word "England" may be there in compliance with the McKinley Tariff Act.

Nantgarw and Swansea Artificial, or Soft Paste, Porcelain (1813–1823)

While the majority of porcelain manufacturers in England were producing bone china during the nineteenth century, two Welsh factories were making soft paste porcelain. This was because a china decorator of special note, William Billingsley (1758–1828), persisted in attempting to produce a soft paste porcelain that would compare with Sèvres. As an arcanist Billingsley was impractical and continued to meet with failure as he shifted from factory to factory.

The Nantgarw porcelain factory was established at the little village of Nantgarw, near Cardiff, Wales, in 1813 by this vagrant porcelain painter. Billingsley had been working as a china painter at Derby, where he first gained notice in 1784 with a new style of painting flowers in which the flowers were first painted in full color, then surplus pigment was wiped off with a dry brush to make highlights. It was not flower painting that interested him, however, but experimenting with soft paste porcelain. At Nantgarw he experienced kiln damage amounting to about nine-tenths, although his wastage on flatwares such as plates may have been quite a bit less since most of the surviving Nantgarw porcelain is in this form. Billingsley decorated some of the output, but a considerable amount was sent to London for decorating to supply the demand for porcelain resembling Sèvres because the accumulated stock was becoming exhausted and no new supplies were being imported.

The Nantgarw factory was moved to Swansea, Wales, in 1814, but Billingsley returned to Nantgarw in 1817 and stayed there until 1819. The Nantgarw factory continued under William Weston Young until 1822, mostly occupied in decorating accumulated stocks of white porcelain. The characteristic decoration consisted of flowers painted in the Billingsley manner, often seen on Derby china, where a number of blossoms composed in groups are realistically rendered in rich coloring. Fruits were treated in the same manner. Billingsley's favorite flowers, which he painted in an admirable manner, were double roses, tulips, lilies, and blooms of brilliant and contrasting colors. A china decorator, Thomas Pardoe, was hired, and he painted birds on branches as well as flowers. In some instances single birds were executed with the exactitude of ornithological illustrations.

The usual mark was NANT-GARW, impressed in the paste, sometimes accompanied by the letters C. W., also impressed. Any mark or marks other than this and any not impressed in the paste should be regarded with distrust. A great deal of spurious Nantgarw china is around.

The Cambrian Pottery at Swansea, South Wales, was founded about 1764 and produced every kind of good-quality earthenware from 1770 to 1870. Much fine underglaze-blue and -black printing was done there, including a series of local views. The Swansea earthenwares of this period compare favorably with and closely resemble those of The Potteries. They are often mistaken for them if unmarked. Ornamental pieces, vases, candlesticks, and lamps, as well as domestic wares, were made in creamware, white earthenware, and black basalt. In 1801 William Dillwyn purchased the lease of the factory. In 1814 he decided Billingsley's porcelain could be a commercial success and the Nantgarw factory was removed to Swansea. Kiln wastage continued, and Dillwyn insisted on modification of the formula, which resulted in a better-quality soft paste body with a marked green translucence. However, the new body was not commercially profitable, and in 1817 soapstone was added to the body. Although Dillwyn transferred his interest, the factory continued under different management using this paste until it closed in 1823. Soft paste tableware, dessert services, and smaller decorative accessories were produced at the Swansea factory, usually decorated with the characteristic "Billingsley" flowers. Ground colors were used, frequently in delicate tones, but besides these there were deep blue, pink, yellow, buff or biscuit, and green.

It is likely that much of the earlier china made at Swansea

Parian ware figure,
probably Copeland, c. 1850.

bore the Nantgarw mark. The Swansea marks were the name SWANSEA impressed in the paste or printed in red, "Dillwyn & Co.," and "Bevinton & Co.," and after 1817 a trident was often impressed in the paste along with the other marks. Fine specimens are much in demand and bring high prices.

Parian Ware

Another porcelain introduced in the nineteenth century was Parian ware. Parian is a hard paste china resembling marble in texture, translucent, with a fine granular surface. It is pleasing to the senses, graceful in form, and divested of glitter. It was given its name because its translucent, creamy surface suggested Parian marble. For this reason it is extensively used for figure modelling.

Copeland & Garrett of Stoke-on-Trent and Minton both claimed to be the first to manufacture Parian. In 1851, an English jury, after receiving statements from both firms, deduced that "whichever party may have actually been first in publicly producing articles in this material they were contemporaneously working with success towards the same results." From the first appearance of the material, a lively competition sprang up between the firms, and it unquestionably proved a source of increased profit and extended reputation to both. It is generally conceded, however, that the invention of Parian should be credited to Copeland of the Spode potteries. He accidentally discovered it while trying to imitate the very fine biscuit of the old Derby factory, the secret of which had long been lost. Copeland produced his first Parian pieces in 1842. It was epoch-making in the history of Staffordshire ceramics. Parian ware became immediately popular and was made not only in England but on the Continent and in America as well. By 1846 it was in commercial production and by 1850 numerous firms were making this body.

XVII

American Porcelain
and Pottery

American porcelain and pottery were not produced with any success or in any quantity until the middle of the nineteenth century. There are many reasons for this, not the least being that the American public simply preferred imported ware. Americans had the fixed idea that foreign art was superior to their own, and refused to buy indigenous attempts at pottery. In fact, the potters did meet with technical failures, since they were trying to use new and unfamiliar clays and glaze materials in combination with methods they had practiced in their homeland pottery industries. The early potters could not afford the expensive experiments necessary to reconcile the two elements, and this made it practically impossible for them to produce good ware.

Accurate records of the wealthier people in America before the Revolution indicate that china was far from plentiful. Only occasionally is an item mentioned, such as in the inventory of the estate of President Davenport of Harvard College in 1648—"Cheyny 4 pounds"—or in the inventory of possessions of Martha Coleymore, who afterward married Governor Winthrop: "One parcel of cheyney plates and saucers 1 pound."

Early settlers in America used wooden trenchers and pewter. Later, Staffordshire wares, such as the mottled glazes of Whieldon and tin-glazed ware from Liverpool and Bristol, were imported into New England. The Dutch settlers in New York (then New Amsterdam) brought in tin-glazed delft. After the middle of the eighteenth century, large amounts of Wedgwood were ordered by Americans, who especially requested "the newest fashion or invention of Mr. Wedgwood."

The trade with China that began with the voyage of the *Empress of China* from New York on February 22, 1784, resulted in enormous quantities of china being shipped into America from the Orient, much by special order. This trade continued throughout the nineteenth century with vast amounts of blue Canton and Nanking being brought into the East Coast ports of the United States. After the War of 1812, the English potters catered to the American trade by making ware that appealed to their patriotism. Meissen and Sèvres porcelain were not imported into America during the eighteenth century to any extent. A large amount of French porcelain was imported from Limoges after the American David Haviland opened a factory there in 1842. Sporadic attempts were made to produce pottery and porcelain in colonial America, which resulted in the production of various earthenwares—redware, stoneware, brownware, and yellowware. The only porcelain that has survived are a few authenticated pieces made at the Bonnin & Morris factory, which was established on Prime Street, Philadelphia, by Gousse Bonnin and George Anthony Morris in 1769. Financial difficulties caused it to close in 1772. Specimens of this factory are extremely rare and are usually in museums.

Tucker China (1825–1838)

The first successful commercial production of porcelain in America was begun in 1825 by William Ellis Tucker in a building known as the Old Waterworks, on Schuylkill Front Street in Philadelphia. He went into this enterprise with the support of his father, Benjamin Tucker, who had been the proprietor of a china shop on High Street, where he had sold choice imported Sèvres and Staffordshire. It was actually a sideline for Benjamin, who was a teacher by profession. Since he lectured in the sciences, he no doubt had knowledge of the ingredients used in porcelain. William Tucker's first step in ceramic art had been decorating the plain pieces received in shipments from abroad and firing them in the back yard of his father's shop. He soon outgrew this and rented the Old Waterworks. From the inception of his resolve to rival the porcelain manufacturers of Europe, Tucker was assiduous not only in kiln experiments but also in his search for ideal material. He was lucky enough to find suitable clays in Delaware, Pennsylvania, and New Jersey.

He attempted twice unsuccessfully to take in partners, but in 1828 Thomas Hulme bought into the firm, and the business was operated under the name of Tucker & Hulme. There are articles in existence inscribed "Tucker & Hulme" with the date 1828.

This firm did not last very long: Hulme died in 1829. The business was prospering to some extent, and a younger brother, Thomas, joined the company and began to learn its different branches. He had a small talent for painting, and his entry into the company improved the quality of the decoration. Extant examples of his paintings are floral studies and minuscule landscapes. Financial and technical difficulties soon began to harass the factory, and aid was sought from the federal government without success. Among those to whom William Ellis Tucker appealed for help was Judge Joseph Hemphill, an important figure in national politics and Philadelphia society who had become interested in the manufacture of porcelain on his trips abroad. Hemphill bought into the firm, expanded the business, and acquired larger properties in May 1831. William Tucker lived only a short time after this, and Judge Hemphill became the sole proprietor when Tucker died in 1832. Hemphill had the good sense to retain Thomas Tucker as factory manager. The judge was alleged to have imported workers from Europe, but it is now concluded that these never arrived, since the existing employee records have no foreign names, nor is there any other evidence to support the idea. (See color insert, Tucker plate.)

The great bank failure of 1833 hit Hemphill so heavily that he could not continue the business. After many attempts to save the works he sold the factory and all its equipment to Joseph Mariner of Boston. Thomas Tucker kept an eye on things during this period, and the kilns never ceased to be fired. Thomas took out a six-month lease from the owners on October 2, 1837. At the end of this period the factory closed.

Thomas Tucker left in the hands of his family the pattern books showing the designs and shapes used at the factory between the years 1832 and 1838. Not all the shapes in the books have been found in identified Tucker china, nor are all the shapes and designs on existing pieces found in the pattern books, but this is not unexpected. There must have been scores of pieces made on special order for a particular client who desired a unique shape for the article ordered, or had in mind some particular pattern to be reproduced. It appears from several of the tea and coffee services still complete that the Tucker factory had been asked to "fill in" pieces from sets originally imported from abroad, or even to develop a whole set from one or two isolated pieces.

Tucker china received a medal in October 1827 from the Franklin Institute at its Fourth Annual Exhibition for "porcelain either plain white or gilt made in Pennsylvania." The Institute was not moved by civic pride when they noted that the ware was superior to the best imported porcelain, because all the products of the Tucker factory from the time William Ellis hit upon the proper combination of materials in the so-called secret formula were harder and consistently finer than the contemporary products from European kilns. Under scrutiny, there is some small variation in color when pieces of Tucker porcelain are held to the light, although the great majority show the greenish tone that has come to be considered typically Tucker. Some doubtful pieces have a decided yellowish cast, perhaps because of a slight difference in the character of the clay taken from neighboring beds.

Tucker china has great heat-resisting qualities, and fire tests show that it stands a higher degree of temperature than Sèvres hard paste of the same period. The paste is very much allied to Sèvres and the finer old Paris porcelain, with which it is often confused. The glaze is clear, transparent, and of a beautiful quality, with a bluish tinge wherever it accumulates in thicker masses near the moldings or in the flutings. The factory output included a variety of objects: table, dessert, tea, and coffee services; inkstands, jardinieres, vases—in fact, all the usual decorative accessories, especially pitchers. The shapes closely copied Sèvres prototypes, and the majority show strong neoclassical influence.

There was a consistency of style in the decoration, all of which was painted, since at no time did the Tucker factory use transfer printing. For this reason it is difficult to assign known pieces to specific periods, although the decoration may be loosely divided into three periods. The first, from 1825 to 1828, consisted of crude monochrome landscapes, butterflies, flowers, and fruits painted in sepia or brown, with gold used only sparingly. During the second period, from 1828 to 1832, Thomas Hulme greatly improved the character of the decoration, including well-executed sprays or groups of flowers and an appropriate degree of gilding. Roses were conspicuous in the bouquets and floral groups. A bird motif was also used. Some objects were done entirely in white and gold and executed with great distinction.

A more ambitious form of decoration was employed in the third period, from 1832 to 1838. In fact the decorating was so well carried out that some Tucker-Hemphill china is mistaken for Sèvres until the mark is examined. Sepia landscapes with gilding and all the flower and bird designs of the second period were continued, but in addition there were table services and vases with festoons, wreaths, or gold tracery surrounding monograms, initials, and occasionally portraits. Roses, tulips, and forget-me-nots were especially dominant in the compact bands and festoons of colored flowers.

Incised initials on the base are considered characteristic of genuine Tucker. These may be in script or block letters. Some are indecipherable. A few correspond to the names of molders known to have been employed at the china factory. They are B, F, H, M, V, and W. The letters A, C, D, K, N, P, U, and X, sometimes found, are unidentified.

Painted marks or inscriptions are much rarer than the incised initials, and it seems that at all periods inscribing was reserved for pieces of particular merit or interest. "William Ellis Tucker," "Tucker & Hulme," "Joseph Hemphill" are the only names recorded to date. No pieces have turned up inscribed "Tucker & Hemphill."

Tucker porcelain is naturally appealing to the American collector. It is the first true porcelain to have been made successfully in America, and is of the finest quality and made in the designs and shapes that particularly attracted Americans in the 1830s—a time when they were strongly influenced by French taste. There is a decided similarity in design and quality to French porcelain of the period 1820–1835. More often than not the two cannot be distinguished by the novice. To add to the confusion Old Paris is often marked with impressed initials, as is Tucker.

The Philadelphia Museum has a good collection of Tucker porcelain and also has the Tucker pattern books. It would be wise to become acquainted with it by sight before paying the steep prices it usually brings. Comparable French porcelain of the same period would be of less value to an American collector. Tucker was produced at one small kiln during thirteen years, whereas Old Paris was produced by many potters over a longer period, and consequently there is far more available on the market.

American Pottery

As early as 1684 a pottery kiln was established in Burlington, New Jersey. Potters are known to have lived in New York, Massachusetts, and Virginia before this date. Probably these potters were producing a soft, porous redware from the local clays. The German colonists in Pennsylvania began to utilize the red, soft-burning clays for pottery soon after settling in eastern Pennsylvania. It was not long before they discovered the white or cream clays of Chester County, from which they produced wares very similar to their south German fathers. The earliest known dated pieces are a platter inscribed "1733" and a sugar bowl with the figure "1742," both accepted as American in spite of their close resemblance to pottery brought from Germany during the same period.

It was necessary to seal the soft, red pottery with a glaze so that it would retain liquids. And, in addition to glaze in various colors, potters decorated this ware in other ways. A quite common ornamentation was produced by incising designs in the soft clay as soon as the piece was made and before glazing, or by crimping the edges of plates and platters in a manner resembling the borders of a piecrust. The Pennsylvania-German potters went further with this method by doing what is technically known as "sgraffito" and was called "scratched wares" by the makers themselves. This method was used for the finest show pieces, mainly plates and platters intended purely for ornament. The designs follow traditional Pennsylvania-Dutch motifs, sometimes even duplicated by stencil: conventionalized tulips, lilies, roses, and pomegranates and occasionally vigorous but crude figures.

Another method of decorating redware was by slip; that is, tracing designs in white or light clay on the red body. In its simplest form, slip decoration consists of lines often waved and frequently parallel with dots as accents. These were sometimes elaborated by touches of green slip, or by forming words. Pie plates, platters, and bowls of this type were made not only in Pennsylvania but also in New Jersey, Maryland, New York, Connecticut, and Ohio.

Redware is charming and interesting but fragile, and the tendency of its soft lead glaze to scale off in everyday use was a serious defect. With increasing knowledge of their natural resources, potters found a sturdier substitute in stoneware. Stoneware clays were found in northern New Jersey and shipped by water to potters as far distant as New Hampshire. By 1800 stoneware came into general use, displacing redware except in small privately owned kilns. For decoration the makers of stoneware relied chiefly on blue or cobalt salts, since this shade was not affected by the high burning temperature of stoneware. The clear, bright blue it produced on various grounds, including shades of gray, buff, and red, rarely varies. The blue coloring was never used as a ground coating but was applied in simple designs —flowers, "feather" scrolls, and conventionalized birds. Such utilitarian articles as churns, jugs, crocks, and bean pots are found in stoneware.

Since stoneware was confined to these heavy, plain vessels, another type of pottery was developed in which more ornamental pieces were made. This is termed "Rockingham," "brownware," and sometimes in Ohio "Queensware." It was produced from fine cream-burning clays, which in the plastic state are smooth enough to be pressed into molds easily and quickly. This body is very similar to crude earthenware, or cream-colored ware. The Americans covered it with brown glazes. This ware was not made by hand. The potters had abandoned the wheel, and the pieces were formed in molds of plaster of Paris. Since this ware was made in the modern type of factory by quantity production methods, it represents a radical departure from earlier types. D. & J. Henderson of Jersey City was making it as early as 1830, and it is best known as the typical ware of the pottery at Bennington, although very large amounts were also produced at Baltimore, Maryland, in the Ohio Valley from Pittsburgh to Cincinnati, and in many other localities. It is possible to make it quite thin and light in weight, so that there are tableware, cups, plates, and bowls as well as modelled ornaments. Such pieces as the gothic-

*"Sally," American red ware with slip decoration,
Pennsylvania, c. 1760.*

patterned sugar or cracker jars made at East Liverpool, Ohio, Bennington's hound-handled pitchers, and the Baltimore "Rebekah-at-the-well" teapot were copied by as many as twelve manufacturers. Consequently makers of unmarked pieces of Rockingham are difficult to identify.

Since the potteries in Bennington, Vermont, were the longest-lived (from 1793 to 1894), the widest variety of types originated there, and other factories—in New England, Pennsylvania, New Jersey, Delaware, the South, and the West—freely copied their models and glazes, Bennington will be used as an example to describe what was being produced in America during this period.

The first factory in Bennington was formed by Captain John Norton in 1793, and the first examples known to have survived from his time are made of redware covered with a slip of lead glaze. Salt-glazed gray stoneware items were produced soon after, the first examples appearing from 1823 to 1828. The early stoneware was decorated with incised patterns or by designs in blue or brown slip. Later, cobalt blue was applied in motifs of flowers, birds, deer, and vines. The best examples were produced between 1840 and 1860. The name "Norton" in slight variations was used as a mark from 1823 to 1894.

Captain John Norton's pottery prospered, and he took his eldest son, Luman, into partnership about 1812. Soon after, another son, John, joined the firm. Captain John Norton handed over the firm to his two sons in 1823, and it continued under the direction of his descendants for over a hundred years.

The second Bennington firm began as an independent operation in 1849 under Christopher Webber Fenton. He was related by marriage to the Norton family, and for a brief span of two years (1845 to 1847) there was a merger of the two potteries.

The Fenton factory manufactured Rockingham-type

brownware, with the mottled dark glaze. Large amounts of pie plates, milk pans, and soap dishes were produced, as well as relief-decorated tableware, pitchers, toby jugs, sugar bowls, and book flasks bearing such ambiguous titles as "Parting Spirits" and "Ladies Companion." Ornamental pieces include figure bottles, candlesticks, lamps, picture frames, curtain tie-backs, and vases copied from a Sandwich-glass celery vase, and culminate in the large and beautifully modelled dogs, deer, and lions that are the masterpieces of Bennington or any other Rockingham ware.

Fenton had the most competent designers and modellers in America, including the famous Daniel Greatbach, an Englishman from a family of potters, who designed the hound-handled pitcher, probably the best-known production of the factory. It was copied extensively by other plants, yet Fenton never thought enough of it to put his factory mark on it, nor to duplicate it in Flint enamel, Parian, or White Granite, as he did many of the other Rockingham models. While at Bennington, Greatbach also copied a toby pitcher he had modelled while he was associated with the Jersey City factory in New Jersey, adding a vine handle.

Fenton made these articles in redware, stoneware, and yellowware (a clear glaze was substituted for the brown), as well, but he liked to experiment and sought to expand the variety of ceramic products he made. He soon began to produce Parian ware and soft and hard paste porcelain.

Parian was introduced at Fenton's pottery in 1848. The modelling of the first Bennington Parian pieces was done by John Harrison, whom the enterprising Fenton brought over from the Copeland Pottery Company in England.

Bennington Parian was composed of flint from Vermont and Massachusetts, feldspar from New Hampshire, and ceramic clays from Vermont and South Carolina, carefully ground and mixed and cast in molds. The term "Parian" is correct only when the piece has no exterior glaze or color so that the resemblance to marble is obvious. However, Bennington Parian pitchers were invariably glazed inside with a clear, transparent glaze. It was either fawn-colored or white. The pitchers are known as the Water Lily, the Knight, the Niagara, the Palm Tree, the Ivy Leaf, and by various other names derived from their decoration. The figure, animal, and bird pieces go by names too—the Samuel, Sheep, Swan, Ram, Bird's Nest, Girl Lacing Shoe, Eagle and Child, Greyhound, and Poodle Dogs. There were also vases, jugs, sugar bowls, creamers, inkwells, knobs, and so on. Plates were made on a very small scale.

The trademark Fenton adopted and used to a limited extent on the Parian ware was a raised scroll or ribbon with the letters USP (United States Pottery Company) impressed and a number indicating the pattern. The articles were also occasionally marked with impressed words on a rectangular frame: "Fenton's Works, Bennington, Vermont."

Fenton made colored porcelain, the most common type being blue-and-white, which was used for pitchers, vases, cologne bottles, and trinket boxes. In the best years of the Fenton pottery, the distinctive blue coloring was obtained by adding oxide of cobalt to some of the slip. Much of the blue-and-white porcelain had a pitted blue background. The pitted surface, which has a close resemblance to orange peel, was laboriously achieved with each pinpoint placed separately on the model by hand. Colored porcelain other than blue-and-white is rare, but examples have been found of several shades of tan-and-white, pink-and-white, and green-and-white.

Fenton began business on his own account, then added several partners. With Oliver A. Gager he formed the United States Pottery Company in 1853. The Fenton factory was closed in 1858, and Fenton moved to Peoria,

Illinois, where he established another factory and continued to make Rockingham, yellowware, and whiteware.

Only about one-fifth of the production of Fenton's pottery was marked in any way. Eight separate marks, in addition to two marks used during the two-year period of the Norton-Fenton partnership, were used. Some of these are indistinguishable, because the impressed mark filled with glaze.

The closing of Fenton's factory in 1858 was only the beginning of the production of pottery and porcelain in this country. Potteries were springing up in new territories as far west as Kaolin, Missouri; a factory was built in Cincinnati, Ohio, in 1862 by Tempest, Brockman and Company. Fenton built a pottery in Peoria, Illinois, which, unlike his Bennington operation, was unsuccessful. Many others were started in New Jersey, South Carolina, New York, and New Orleans, among other locations. Most of these turned out to be comparatively unimportant, and almost all of them were more or less temporary.

The first successful manufacturers of whiteware (white-bodied earthenware) in the country congregated at Trenton, New Jersey, where they specialized in White Granite and the cheaper cream-colored ware. White Granite had been introduced about 1850, and describes a dense, almost vitreous body, pure white in color and without decoration. The Trenton potteries include Taylor and Speeler, William Young & Sons, and Millington and Astbury. By 1864, there were twelve potteries in Trenton.

After 1880, many American potters made "art pottery" of one type or another. White Granite was improved by James Pass of the Onandaga Pottery at Syracuse, New York, into vitrified china about 1888. The body was similar —opaque and vitreous—but lighter and more graceful in shape. Other types of ware were introduced. Some makers made considerable changes in the body of Parian, so that it was no longer Parian but an unglazed, or biscuit, porcelain differing from the original in color and texture, being whiter and coarser. The designs used were most inappropriate to marble, particularly pitchers, which for utility's sake were given a coat of glaze on the interior. After 1883, a modification of Parian appeared, a very thin, light-cast ware, slightly washed with pearly metallic lusters. This is known as "Belleek," from the pottery in Ireland where it was first made. It was introduced in the United States by Ott and Brewer of Trenton.

Belleek Porcelain

Belleek porcelain was first exhibited by the Belleek Porcelain Factory, Ireland, at the Dublin International Exhibition of 1865, and was produced throughout the latter part of the nineteenth century. Belleek, a remarkably thinly potted porcelain, covered with a distinctive iridescent glaze, is noted for its beauty and skillful modelling. Many articles were made in the form of shells and corals, and considerable imagination was bestowed on openwork baskets encrusted with flowers. Some Belleek combines an unglazed body similar to Parian with the usual lustrously glazed body, which results in a very interesting effect.

Belleek was soon made by several of the better potters in the United States, but Ott and Brewer Company, of Trenton, who introduced it, excelled in the production. By 1882, they had mastered a sophisticated decoration of molded and applied flowers that had an Oriental tone. Typical marks used by this factory are "Manufactured by /Ott & Brewer/Trenton, N.J. USA," and a crown pierced by a sword with "Belleek" above and "O & B" below.

The Ceramic Art Company, which was started in 1889 by Walter Scott Lenox, was another well-known Trenton pottery that made superior Belleek as well as other fine porcelain. One of its more familiar Belleek creations is a swan dish, which was produced about 1890. This firm was renamed Lenox Inc. in 1906 and is known by that name the world over. Typical marks for their products are "The Ceramic Art Co., Trenton, N.J.," enclosed within a wreath, and a highly stylized C A C enclosed within an oval with a painter's palette and brushes to the left.

Still another Trenton pottery producing Belleek was the Willetts Manufacturing Company. The most important pieces made at this factory during the late 1880s and 1890s are notable for the delicacy and restraint of their floral decoration. The typical mark was a snake coiled to form a W with "Belleek" above and "Willetts" below.

In the 1880s Taylor and Knowles Company, established in 1872 in East Liverpool, Ohio, developed a porcelain as thin and translucent as Belleek, which was called "Lotus ware." Each article was individually designed, executed, and decorated—a method quite different from the usual practice of the day. This firm used Oriental shapes, but also leaned toward the revival of Renaissance or rococo styles. A vase exhibited at the Chicago Exhibition has its entire surface covered with an underglaze mazarine blue of a rich tone. On one side is a figure of Cupid chasing a bird, and on the other of Cupid driving a pair of butterflies. The treatment was original, with the figures built up in white over the glaze, instead of under it, in the *pâte-sur-pâte* method, causing a most pleasing effect. The mark was generally "Knowles, Taylor and Knowles" within a circle surrounding a crescent and star, with "Lotus Ware" beneath the circle. This porcelain was among the best produced anywhere in America at this time.

In New York, with its large and prosperous buying public, there were several manufacturers of fine pottery, none
particularly successful. However, one of the first really successful art potteries made in America was produced in
New York. This was the hard-fired pinkish terra-cotta made
by John Rogers from 1860 until about 1890—large figures
and groups which he molded from this material, covered
with drab-colored paint, and termed "Rogers' Groups."
These could be found on all stylish parlor tables for a generation or more. In spite of having been pressed in molds,
they showed considerable technical skill. These figures,
imbued with saccharine mid-Victorian sentimentality, were
actually modelled by some talented sculptors, notably Daniel Chester French. The factory also produced large and
fine figures in white Parian. John Rogers proved to be of
some importance in American ceramic history.

Art Pottery (1870–1900)

There was a widespread interest in pottery decoration in
the decade following the Philadelphia Centennial. Americans were beginning to feel the effects of William Morris'
Arts and Crafts Movement in England, and potters wished
to design new forms and decorate them in an original manner. It became the vogue for amateurs to decorate ceramics.
Beginning as an amusement of the rich, it soon became an
industry. The trend was assisted by potters teaching the
craft in the new schools that were opening in the East and
Midwest to train artisans, and it is not surprising that a
number of attempts to establish art potteries were made at
this time. One of the first was in Cincinnati, Ohio. Here in
1874, Ben Pitman formed a class for instruction in the art
of painting on china. The enthusiasm of the group was

quickly expressed and the class prepared some specimens to be shown at the Philadelphia Centennial. These received high praise from the press and art critics, and the class developed into what was later called the Rookwood Pottery.

The person largely responsible for starting Rookwood was Mrs. Maria Longworth Nichols (later Mrs. Bellamy Storer) of Cincinnati. By 1875, she was enthusiastically furthering the interests of china painting among amateurs, although at the same tme promoting it as a "promising field for the lucrative employment of women." She was further inspired by the ceramic display from Japan at Philadelphia in 1876. The Rookwood Pottery was founded in 1880 in Cincinnati and soon became the foremost art pottery manufacturer in America. It remained so for the next half century. Her father, who was wealthy and a patron of the arts, furnished the necessary means for the maintenance of the factory until it could stand on its own feet financially, which it did until production was curtailed and controlling interest was sold in the summer of 1967, when the operation of Rookwood Pottery was suspended.

No ceramic establishment in the United States has come nearer to fulfilling the requirements of a distinctive American institution than the Rookwood Pottery. It is also appealing that the founding of the factory was due to the intelligent and well-directed efforts of a woman. Rookwood wares continue to enjoy increasing popularity as collectibles.

During 1881 the pottery produced several thousand pieces in seventy to ninety different shapes. Some of these models were later abandoned when they proved too difficult to handle or were found unsalable. The first productions were commercial wares for table and household purposes, including considerable quantities of breakfast and dinner services, pitchers, plaques, vases, wine coolers, ice tubs, water buckets, and umbrella jars. The body was halfway between cream-colored and White Granite ware.

*Rookwood vase, dull-finished gray with color-enamelled
flower spray. Marked on the base with the Chinese-character
mark of Laura A. Frye and Rookwood's monogram mark of 1886.*

A variety of popular patterns used transparent underglaze blue and brown prints of birds, fish, and other animal subjects on ivory. These early artistic designs are now difficult to procure and are much sought after. Every form made in white during this early period was also made in blue, sage green, and red, and pieces were frequently ornamented with devices carved in the paste.

Printing was soon abandoned and superseded by the more elegant painted decorative forms that now attract so much attention. Mrs. Nichols produced work of a high artistic order after the Japanese style. The new methods adopted were original, and all copying was discontinued. A device similar to a mouth atomizer for spraying fixative on charcoal drawings was employed; it was first used by Laura Fry to apply colored slips to the green clay body of a piece she was decorating. The evenness of application and delicate shading of color was far superior to that possible with a brush and was particularly good for applying background colors. Colored glazes were thereafter used with greater frequency and better effect, and decorative designs were based more on floral subjects. This underglaze ware, earlier called "Limoges," became Standard Rookwood as the pottery developed its distinctive style. M. Louise McLaughlin was one of the women in the original china-painting class who continued to work with Mrs. Nichols. She developed "Losanti ware," a hard paste porcelain fired at a low temperature and glazed with feldspar. Because of its high vitreous quality, some of her pieces resemble glass.

The pottery employed other exceptionally fine artists as decorators, among whom were Albert R. Valentien, Matt A. Daly, and Kataro Shirayamadani, a Japanese artist who did some of the finest work using Oriental methods. E. P. Cranch was a clever artist who did humorous sketches in black and brown. He had a quaint style that is seen at its best in a set of mantel tiles painted by him to illustrate the old American ballad "Isaac Abbott," and in a similar series of titles illustrating the ancient ballad of "Giles Scroggins' Ghost." He also decorated a variety of other pieces, such as beer mugs and pitchers.

Most Rookwood bodies rely on the natural color of the clay for their tint, but sage green and pink were artificially produced with mineral colors. The ware manufactured at Rookwood was of three types:

CAMEO, or shell-tinted, ware, generally a beautiful pink color, gradually shading into white and highly glazed.

DULL FINISHED ware, similar in color to the former, but possessing a surface soft in texture and having the appearance of being unglazed.

ROOKWOOD FAIENCE, the most characteristic of all, a richly glazed ware, a natural or artificially colored body covered with an opaque glaze.

The distinguishing feature of all Rookwood is the tinting and harmonious blending of the ground colors beneath the heavy, transparent, colored glazes, producing rich tones of black, yellow, red, olive, green, brown, and amber of great brilliancy, mellowness, depth, and strength.

Rookwood pottery from the beginning was influenced by Oriental designs to a large degree in shape, decoration, and glaze. There was also a strong influence of naturalism, and the beginnings of art nouveau are noticeable in many of the pieces.

Identification of Rookwood art pottery started with the pieces prepared for the first kiln in 1880. Until 1882 various marks were employed to identify the factory. These are found incised or painted on the bottom of each piece. The first mark used was the name ROOKWOOD, painted in gold, together with the initials of the decorator, Maria Longworth Nichols. The ware was not dated. In 1881 the most common mark was the name of the pottery incised in the base, usually accompanied by the date. From 1882 to 1886 the mark was an impressed monogram R P and the year.

The R–P monogram mark, first used on June 23, 1886, became the standard mark, replacing the word ROOKWOOD on ware made after that date. To represent the year 1887, one flame point was placed above the R–P. Another flame point was added for each year until there were fourteen flame points for the year 1900. The R–P mark with fourteen flame points was continued into the new century with the addition of a Roman numeral to denote the year. After 1962, R in a circle was sometimes added to denote that the trademark was registered. There are many other marks, symbols, and decorators' signatures.

With the success of Rookwood other attempts were made to establish art potteries. Many of these were short-lived.

W. A. Long of Steubenville, Ohio, was one of the first to try with what was called "Lonhuda ware," but he soon moved to the pottery operated by S. A. Weller in Zanesville, Ohio. At the World's Columbian Exposition in 1893 Weller had been so impressed with the Rookwood art pottery that he decided to enter the field. He acquired Long's Lonhuda Company and produced the ware under the name "Louwelsa." This name was usually impressed on the bottom of the article. He fabricated pottery that closely resembled Rookwood Standard wares, with underglaze decorations of flowers, fruits, portraits of American Indians, and animals done on spray-blended grounds of darker colors.

Weller also expanded his art pottery production by the addition of new styles. By 1904 he had included Aurelian, which was similar to Louwelsa, though the background was applied by brush rather than spray-painted; Eocean, also similar, but with a lighter body color and lighter and more delicate backgrounds shaded with the atomizer; Dickensware, usually incised designs filled in with color, or scenes from the work of Charles Dickens done in this technique; Sicardo, characterized by metallic luster designs on iridescent dark-green, brown, and purple backgrounds applied to many forms, distinctly a different and original technique; Turada, a white waxlike decoration on a very dark or black ground; and L'Art Nouveau, a semimat finish, usually decorated in relief design.

The name "Weller" was impressed on the bottom of the ware. Around 1932, when the company was suffering from the Depression and hand-decorating was virtually discontinued, "Weller" appeared in a script style of lettering. The S. A. Weller Company was officially dissolved on August 18, 1949.

The J. B. Owens Company, operating in Roseville, Ohio, also made ware closely resembling Rookwood's Standard ware and Weller's Louwelsa. The firm used a number of designs in underglaze slip painting on both light and dark grounds. The Roseville Pottery Company started in business in 1892 by acquiring the original J. B. Owens plant in Roseville. It introduced new lines with increasing frequency to meet the competition. After going through many changes of production, finally on November 1, 1954, the Roseville pottery closed.

Marks include the name ROZANNE WARE and a rose. Also the incised name ROZANE and the letters R. P. Co. (for Roseville Pottery Company). The incised ROZANE mark is believed to have been in use until about 1905 or 1906. The R P CO, sometimes used earlier in conjunction with the ROZANE mark, was used alone until about 1910.

Ceramics from the art potteries in America have become vastly collectible. They represent what a group of artistically inclined individuals created to combat the quantities of rather inferior mass-produced wares of the Industrial Revolution. American art pottery deservedly brings high prices. Be sure not to confuse it with the factory-made ceramics of the same period that still flood the market.

XVIII

Advice to the Novice

Novice collectors often begin by buying any and every piece that appeals to them which they think is reasonably priced. In this way, it is possible to squander a large sum of money and have nothing of value to show for it. On the other hand, a comparatively small amount of money may be spent accompanied with an infinite amount of care and attention and result in a collection of importance. Porcelain and pottery is a complex subject, and mastery of the field requires a considerable amount of reading and study and the practice of examining hundreds of specimens. The suggestions in this book should give the beginner the practical training and basic knowledge he requires, but he must also educate his eye to recognize the good and the bad.

How can the beginner learn to discriminate? Essentially by developing the critical sense and confidence that grow out of knowledge. Most people think good taste is something you are born with, but it can be acquired. A person who enjoys painting gathers a sense of fine production and learns to distinguish the good from the bad by repeated visits to museums, galleries, exhibitions, and great collections. It is the same with anyone who has an instinctive love for porcelain or pottery. He can gain experience, knowledge, taste, and judgment by frequenting museums that have galleries of quality ceramics that are well classified. Visit these, and also visit antique shops whose experienced owners have their authentic articles well displayed. These dealers are only too anxious to talk to you about their choice porcelain and to "educate" you on the subject: the different types of decoration, the good factories, and how to read the marks. It is to their advantage to recruit more knowledgeable buyers and collectors. It is a pity that the beginner is often embarrassed to go into fine shops because the façade frightens him. He will, instead, go into a small shop, feeling more at ease and also thinking he will find a bargain, but he will probably be confronted by an uninformed dealer of little experience who has inferior stock, and nothing is gained.

When a beginner starts learning, he should acquire one good piece with the guidance of a reliable and knowledgeable dealer or friend. Place it where it can be constantly seen. Place next to it an article you are considering buying, and even a collector of moderate experience will recognize without doubt whether it is a fraud or an inferior object. There is no more severe test for a sham than to be placed in the company of the real thing. It is also good to buy a cracked or damaged piece occasionally because it can teach you something about paste, glaze, decoration, or modelling. Attention to these details makes for connoisseurship. In addition, constant study, intelligence, and experience must be depended upon to protect the young collector from being deceived.

An open mind is absolutely essential in judging or identifying porcelain and pottery. A preconceived idea will blind you to observing the various factors that must be considered in making a correct attribution. A beginner attempting a proper identification should start by eliminating all classes of ware in which it positively cannot belong. Gradually the field becomes limited to one period and country and finally narrows down to two or three factories. Then, it is only with practice and study that a definite and accurate conclusion can be reached.

The first matter to determine when attempting an identification is ordinarily easy: that is, is it an article of porcelain or pottery? Holding the object up to a strong light reveals, in most cases, whether it is opaque or translucent. If it is translucent it is undoubtedly porcelain. You might also tap it lightly to test it for a clear ring. Porcelain usually does give a ring, although this is not always accurate. Porcelain that has been repaired, even though the repair may not be perceptible, will not ring. In addition, hard paste opaque wares, such as Wedgwood's fine jaspers, will sound a clear ring when struck.

Then comes the question that stumps many experienced collectors as well as the beginner: Is it hard paste, soft paste, or bone china? This is an important decision, since the answer immediately gives a clue to the country of manufacture. Having an example of each type of paste, preferably a broken piece where paste is more visible, is the most advantageous way to check and compare. Soft paste seems to be the most puzzling and the most difficult to identify. Scratch the base of an article, which generally has no glaze, with a file (I often use my fingernail). If it can be marked with a file it is soft paste. Also, where it is chipped it can be seen that the body is granular. Use a scrubbing brush and clean off the base thoroughly; the dirt will not come off a piece made of soft paste, since it has soaked into the porous body; on hard paste ware the dirt will come off with scrubbing. What a difference proper washing makes to a piece of china, even an apparently clean one! The glaze of soft paste porcelain in particular is always somewhat scratched, and the minute scratches collect dirt. A simple method of cleaning is to rub household ammonia gently over the surface with cotton wool, which completely removes every trace of the dirt, then soak it in any good washing liquid with a little ammonia added, rinse it in clean tepid water, and set it on blotting paper to dry.

I will not repeat the various details to consider when making an identification of porcelain or pottery here, since they are given in Chapter IV and throughout the book, but it has often been remarked that the surest way to get together a bad collection of ceramics is to rely on the marks, because they can cause a great deal of confusion if taken at face value. If all the characteristics of a specimen taken together are in favor of a certain attribution, then a confirming mark is a valuable piece of conclusive evidence. By itself, however, and without the essential characteristics, a mark guarantees nothing. A collector of ceramics should get to know his subject so well that he really doesn't need the mark to make an identification.

There is some further information on English marks that might be of assistance. In English wares of the nineteenth century, there are certain often-used forms of marks that can facilitate in determining the approximate date:

Any printed marks incorporating the Royal Arms (or versions of the arms) are nineteenth-century or later.
Any printed mark incorporating the name of the pattern is subsequent to 1810.

Use of the word "Royal" in the manufacturer's title or trade
name suggests a date after the middle of the nineteenth
century. Example: "Royal Worcester."

The words "Bone China" or "English Bone China" denote a
twentieth-century date.

"England" was added to marks from 1891 to comply with the
American McKinley Tariff Act.

"Made in England" signifies a twentieth-century date. The use
of "Limited" in various abbreviations—"Ld," "Ltd"—after
a pottery firm's title indicates a date after 1860.

The use of the words "Trade Marks" signifies a date subsequent
to the Trade-Mark Act of 1862, and usually denotes a date
after 1875.

The diamond registration mark was used from 1843 to 1883.

The use of "Rd. No." followed by a number signifies a date after
1884; if the number is above 360,000, the date is after 1900.

Some fraudulent or imitation marks of specific factories
have been shown in the preceding text, but there will be
others that a beginner may come across and by which he
may be deceived.

The most blatantly falsified mark is that of the Capo
di Monte factory. The real old Capo di Monte wares made
in Naples were seldom if ever marked. The models were
bought by Marquis Ginori long after the early factories
became extinct, and he established a factory near Florence,
where majolica of a decorative character and also porcelain
were made, which he marked with the letter N surmounted
by a coronet, either in blue or scratched in the paste. The
scratched or incised N is as a rule considered better and
older work than that bearing the blue mark.

There are other imitations of old Capo di Monte on
the market. These are coarse, badly finished productions of
French and German firms, generally tankards, vases, and
bowls of an ambitious and pretentious character, and they

generally bear the letter mark N surmounted by a coronet, sometimes in gold, but more frequently in blue. They are to be avoided as quite worthless from a collector's point of view. These have been manufactured in enormous quantities.

There are some imitations made to deceive that are so perfect they are difficult to detect. Fortunately, their very perfection and supposed rarity takes them out of the reach of all but the very wealthy. If you wish to invest in a fine piece, go to a knowledgeable dealer of integrity and on purchase get a bill or invoice of sale with full description and the understanding that if it turns out not to be authentic it can be returned. An invoice is also important for maintenance of records and for insurance.

Occasionally one is confronted with the puzzling situation, especially in a dinner or tea set, of finding on close examination that the pieces are not all from the same factory. The explanation for this is that the owner, wishing to have broken pieces replaced, would send a piece to a factory to be duplicated, and if the factory was no longer in existence or not convenient, the article would then be sent to a different factory. In checking a first-period Worcester tea set, I found that some of the articles were hard paste and had been made at a Paris factory. This was no intentional deception; however, it does influence the price. Occasionally these "filled in" dinner sets come up at auction and should be examined carefully and that fact considered when bidding.

It is all right to buy a restored or damaged article if you are aware of it, either recognizing the condition yourself or being told about it by the dealer, but you do not want to buy an impaired article under the impression that it is in proof condition and pay for it accordingly. Even if a repair cannot be perceived at first glance, it can sometimes be detected with closer scrutiny. If it is a recent repair, you can often detect the scent of paint by smelling it. What has been the surer way until recently is that if a known piece of porcelain is tapped and does not resound with a ring, it has been repaired. Now there appear to be repairers who can put together an article that has been broken in many pieces and have it still ring.

If you find a damaged or repaired article you want for your collection and the price is not too high, I recommend buying it, and perhaps later, with luck, it can be replaced with a perfect piece. Also consider where it is to be displayed. I have a very early Chinese Export punch bowl with most of the back missing. It is placed on the top shelf of a corner cupboard and blends beautifully in the room and gives out no clues to being damaged.

When a damaged article of very good and rare quality is acquired, it is advisable to have it repaired by a good china repairer. In most cases the damage won't be noticeable, and often the price for restoring is not too high. With less-valuable pieces, use sure hands and a home method and the result will often prove very satisfactory.

Only the experienced collector can hope nowadays to pick up bargains in a thrift shop, a junk shop, a general antique shop, or an auction. As more dealers' knowledge of china and awareness of current market values increases, they regularly scour every small concern, however remote, and no country sale is neglected by them.

Until a beginner has gained knowledge, he should not expect to buy cheaply in a general antique shop. The wise collector is willing to buy from a reliable and knowledgeable dealer, confident that what he buys is what it is claimed to be, and paying not only for the article but also for the seller's knowledge, information, the trouble he has taken to find his stock, and the guarantee that goes with the purchase. Once a dealer of this sort has the confidence of his customer, he will help him find the kind of pieces he ought to have, at the right price, and will tactfully guide his attention away from anything that is unworthy of "The Collection." An added advantage is that a dealer of repute is always willing to take back anything that later proves not to be what was claimed. If a purchase made at auction, country sale, or thrift shop turns out to be broken, skillfully restored, or not authentic, there is no recourse.

There is always great excitement and a feeling of anticipation upon attending an auction, whether it is a New England country auction or one conducted at a major gallery in a big city, and it is possible to become so carried away that you will bid on unimportant objects. Try instead to set yourself a firm limit in line with current prices, and don't exceed it, however great the temptation. It is usually possible to view the articles prior to the sale. If it is a catalogued sale, the catalogue will not state the condition or age. That can only be determined by examining the article before it comes on the block. The stock to be sold is often out on display several days before the sale, but in case it is not convenient to see it during that time, the big galleries allow you to come behind the scenes just before the sale to handle and view the items. If you decide to bid, do it with an informed person who can advise you. At the larger auctions you will have the competition of some of the most experienced buyers, ones with plenty of financial backing. Only occasionally can you pick up a real bargain. However, sometimes a typical mixed sale of ceramics offers such a wide choice that although goods of exceptional quality will always command a very high price, the more ordinary articles—still worthwhile and desirable—may be bought reasonably. For example, at a sale that advertised fine collections of extraordinary examples of Wedgwood, first-period Worcester, and Leeds, some dessert sets of nineteenth-century bone china were also included. As the majority of buyers came to bid on the Wedgwood, Worcester, and Leeds, the colorfully decorated bone china of the 1830s went for a very low price.

What to collect? That depends on the individual's taste, desires, and pocketbook, but it should be something appealing from an aesthetic and technical point of view. It does not have to be all one category, such as a group of Staffordshire animals, or pitchers of various styles and sizes. A collection may contain a variety of objects of one class of porcelain or pottery representative of different kinds of English blue-and-white soft paste, American-historic Staffordshire, or Chinese Export. It can be even more comprehensive by including good-quality ceramics of particular merit from different countries and periods. The result can be an accumulation of specimens of beauty and worth that will be enjoyable and educational. This type of collection gives the buyer more freedom in selecting articles that represent the good points of different manufactures at a reasonable price.

When buying porcelain and pottery, always consider an object for its intrinsic excellence and beauty. It does not always have to be judged by its age. If high standards are kept in mind, it can be advantageous to branch out into a field not yet overworked or one newly discovered. New things become old and take their turn as antiques, and each succeeding generation brings its own contingent of collectors.

The main thing is to enjoy yourself while studying, learning, and collecting. Then you will be rewarded not only by pleasing objects and an absorbing hobby but also by the many new friends you will have made.

Glossary

ABSOLON, WILLIAM (1751–1815). A pottery decorator and china and glass dealer at Yarmouth. About 1790 he set up a pottery-decorating business known as "The Ovens," where he enamelled earthenware and porcelain bought in the white from Staffordshire and Leeds. Absolon's mark, "Absolon Yarme No. 25," painted in red, occurs on wares bought from Turner, Wedgwood, Shorthose, and Leeds and impressed with their marks.

ACANTHUS. The most widely used plant form in the decorative arts. Both the leaf and flower were employed in all forms of decoration, including ceramics.

AGATE. A ware resembling agate or marble, made by wedging together clays of several colors, thereby extending them through the body, or by painting the surface of the piece with mixed colors. Brown tones generally predominated.

ALBARELLO. A word of obscure derivation used to describe the nearly cylindrical majolica drug pot introduced into Italy from Spain and later copied by English makers of tin-glazed earthenware.

ALCOCK & CO., SAMUEL. The firm began business as the Hill Pottery, Burslem, Staffordshire, in 1831. As Alcock & Co., manufactured good-quality porcelain, bisque figures modelled from historical subjects, and Parian vases and figures until 1859, when the company failed.

AMORINI. Also called *putti* and "small boys." Figures of Cupid or winged cupid's heads, derived from Roman sources and often portrayed in porcelain.

AMPHORA. A two-handled Greek vessel for holding wine, oil, corn, or honey. In shape a graceful footed ovoid, with flaring trumpet-shaped neck and bold lip, the opening wide enough to hold a ladle. Made extensively in the Rhineland from c. 720 to c. 1190 as containers for the Rhine wine exported to Britain and to Baltic countries.

ANGOULÊME FAIENCE. This factory in the suburb of Houmeau was started about 1748. Typical of the productions were large faience animals—lions, dogs, cats, or sphinxes—with heavy manganese outlines to their features.

ANSBACH FAIENCE AND PORCELAIN. Founded in 1710 and extended in 1757 for the making of porcelain.

APOSTLE JUG. A straight-sided jug modelled in relief with figures of the Apostles under an elaborate gothic arcading, made by Charles Meigh in porcelaneous stoneware, c. 1845.

AQUAMANILE. A water-holding vessel, usually in the form of a mounted knight or animal.

ARABESQUE. A form of surface ornament composed of light scroll-work and foliage of an intricate kind, sometimes covering the entire surface.

ARCANIST. A workman professing to have the secret (arcanum) of making porcelain or of some kinds of pottery, notably faience, during the eighteenth century.

ARITA. A Japanese area, Hizen Province, where Japanese porcelain was made in forty-odd factories.

ART NOUVEAU. Essentially a resurgence of the romantic aesthetic, expressing itself in decoration based upon plant rhythm characterized in form and "ornament" by intense and sinuous lines and curves. The style was adopted by many ceramic artists in the late nineteenth and early twentieth centuries.

ASHWORTH, G. L., & BROTHERS (LTD.). Broad Street, Hanley, Staffordshire, potters, 1862. Made earthenwares, ironstone, etc. Succeeded Francis Morley.

ASTBURY WARES. A term used to describe a number of Staffordshire wares presumably made by John Astbury (1686–1743) and his son, Thomas, or wares in that style. The most important use a red clay that has been ornamented with applied and stamped reliefs in white clay, the whole covered with a lead glaze.

ASTBURY-WHIELDON WARES. Staffordshire wares in the "Astbury" style, but covered with the mottled glaze characteristic of Thomas Whieldon.

AYNSLEY, JOHN, & SONS (LTD.). Portland Works, Longton, Staffordshire (1864 to present). Makers of porcelain.

BADDELEY, JOHN & EDWARD. Shelton, Staffordshire. Potters (1784–

1806) producing earthenwares. They used impressed marks of initials and BADDELEY.

BADDELEY, WILLIAM. Eastwood, Hanley, Staffordshire potteries (1802–1822). Made earthenwares of Wedgwood type, caneware, black basalt, etc., engine-turned. The mark "Eastwood" was impressed.

BARKER, SAMUEL, & SON. Don Pottery, Swinton, North Rotherham, Yorkshire (1843–1893). Earthenwares. Used impressed mark "Barker Don Pottery," c. 1834.

BELL, J. & M. P., & CO. (LTD.). Glasgow pottery, Dobbies Loan, Glasgow, Scotland (1842–1928), making earthenwares, Parian, etc. A mark of bell shapes impressed or printed, with or without initials B or J. B.

BELLARMINE. An almost pear-shaped salt-glazed stoneware wine jug with a short, narrow neck on which is a molded mask thought in England to be a caricature of the hated Cardinal Bellarmine (1542–1621), or of the Duke of Alva. These bottles were called Bartmannkrüge (bearded-man jugs) when made at Cologne au Raeren, Germany, and stoneware of this kind in Elizabethan England was generally known as "tyger ware." Bellarmines were copied in the nineteenth century by Hubert Schiffer of Raeren, who stamped his initials in the base. Specimens with a ground patch that suggests the remount of stamped initials are probably spurious.

BIANCO SOPRA BIANCO. A term describing white over white. Decoration in white on a tin-glazed ware. Found on sixteenth-century majolica, Nevers, and Marieberg faience, and on English Bristol delft of the eighteenth century.

BIDET. A low stool, usually covered, holding a metal or pottery basin of violin shape, and principally used for feminine hygiene. The bidet had its origins in France, where it was to be found almost universally in the eighteenth century as almost an object of ceremony, ladies apparently holding court and receiving guests while enjoying its comforts. In consequence it was frequently elaborately decorated, and occasionally wittily inscribed.

BING & GRONDAHL. A porcelain manufactory established by Harold Bing in 1853 in Copenhagen, which quickly achieved a reputation for porcelain, stoneware, and earthenware, eventually rivalling the productions of the Royal Porcelain Factory.

BIRCH, EDMUND, JOHN, AND SHELTON. The firm, recorded in 1802, made excellent black basalt and jasper wares in the Wedgwood style. They have the impressed mark BIRCH or "Birch." The factory was sold in 1818.

BISCUIT PORCELAIN. An unglazed porcelain that was introduced in 1751 and became very popular. The fashion revived during the nineteenth century, when it was called Parian ware. First marketed about 1845.

BLACK-GLAZED POTTERY. Red earthenware covered with a lustrous black or brownish glaze. Made in Staffordshire at Fenton Vivian by Whieldon, Jackfield, and others.

BLANC DE CHINE. The name given to a certain type of Chinese porcelain by Jesuit missionaries. A fine white porcelain with a glaze richer than the normal feldspathic glaze of the imperial factories. It was made at Te-hua (Fukien Province) in southern China.

BLEU CÉLESTE. A turquoise-blue ground color introduced at the Vincennes porcelain factory in 1752.

BLEU DE ROI. A strong, very even blue enamel introduced at Sèvres a little before 1760.

BOCAGE. The term is used in decorative arts principally to describe the background of branches, bushes, and flowers on English and German porcelain figures in the rococo style. Elaborate bocage, often of the maybush, is characteristic of the best English figures of the 1760s.

BOUCHER, FRANÇOIS (1703–1770). A French painter and designer, who reflected the rather frivolous but voluptuous taste of the time and greatly influenced design in the decorative arts until about 1770. He inspired porcelain figures made at Chelsea and Meissen. Subjects of his paintings are to be found on the early porcelain of Vincennes and Sèvres.

BOURDALOU. A name applied to a convenient portable article of feminine toilette. It was carried by ladies concealed in their muffs as an emergency during the long hours at court and at church. In form it corresponds with the coach pot.

BUEN RETIRO PORCELAIN FACTORY. This Spanish porcelain factory, a continuation of Capo di Monte, was started in 1760. It was situated near Madrid, and the products are rarely seen outside Spain.

C AND S SCROLLS. Ornament approximately in the form of the letters C and S, which is a special feature of the rococo style.

CABARET SET. A porcelain service made for one or two people with porcelain tray to match.

CABBAGE-LEAF JUGS. Jugs, originally made at Worcester, with overlapping leaves in relief, *c.* 1757. Later made at Lowestoft and Caughley.

CADDY. A small box or receptacle to contain tea. Porcelain and pottery versions are sometimes termed "tea jars."

CADOGAN TEAPOT. A teapot derived from a Chinese winepot of peach shape, which had no opening at the top and was filled through the bottom. This was first made at Rockingham with its brown glaze and later made elsewhere.

CAEN, CALVADOS, FRANCE. A hard paste porcelain made *c.* 1793–1806 in the Sèvres Empire style using colored grounds with gilding and painting. The mark: CAEN stencilled in red.

CAMAÏEU, EN. A decoration in several shades and intensities of the same color used on porcelain and wall decoration.

CAMPANA VASE. A vase made in the neoclassic style, during the first decade of the nineteenth century. Derived from *campana*, a church bell, hence bell-shaped.

CAN, CANN. A straight-sided cup or mug, with or without handles, for coffee, chocolate, or punch, made in porcelain, pottery, and silver.

CANEWARE. Buff-colored ware introduced by Wedgwood in 1779 for useful and ornamental pieces. Also called "piecrust" and "bamboo" ware.

CAPO DI MONTE PORCELAIN FACTORY. This Naples factory was started in 1743 under the patronage of Charles, King of Naples. The body used was a kind of soft paste porcelain, usually slightly cream in color. Both figures and serviceware are very rare. Capo di Monte porcelain is usually unmarked, but it sometimes bears, in common with Buen Retiro, the fleur-de-lis. In the past a great deal of hard paste porcelain decorated with figure subjects in relief, enamelled in colors, has been falsely attributed to Capo di Monte.

CARRARA. Nineteenth-century trade term for a Wedgwood white hard paste porcelain body resembling white Carrara marble. Also termed Parian ware.

CARTOUCHE. A frame sometimes used to enclose scenes, views, portraits, floral groups, birds, etc., much used in the decoration of pottery and porcelain, particularly in the rococo period, when it took on a fantastic shape and was elaborately embellished with scrolls and foliage.

CARYATIDS. Supporting members shaped like women in the dress of the Caryan people who were taken captive by the Athenians.

CASSOLETTES. Vases of porcelain or metal with a pierced cover, usually intended as pastille burners. In the eighteenth century the covers were often reversible, one side being fitted with a candleholder.

CAULIFLOWER WARE. Green- and yellow-glazed earthenware made in the form of cauliflowers, pineapples, and other vegetables, by Whieldon, Wedgwood, and others from 1750 on. Cauliflowers were also made in porcelain at Chelsea and Longton Hall.

CAVETTO. The deep center part of a dish, plate, or platter.

CELADON GLAZE. True Chinese celadon results from covering a stoneware body with a ferruginous slip before adding a feldspathic glaze. Subsequent firing produces a color that is usually a valued shade of green. However, true celadon can be variable in shade and range from putty color through greens of various shades to olive.

CERAMICS. From the Greek *keramos*, a potter's earth, this term is generally applied to any material made of fired clay.

CHALKWARE (1850–1890). A name given in America to mantel ornaments made of plaster of Paris in imitation of the more expensive pottery and porcelain figures popular in the eighteenth and nineteenth centuries. Subjects were usually made in pairs—cats, dogs, cockerels, sheep, goats, and especially doves and fruit pyramided in urns.

CHANTILLY SPRIG. A light, airy pattern consisting of graceful sketchy sprays of flowers, twigs, grasses, or ears of corn, sometimes painted in dual crimson, manganese, purple, and brown, but much more often in blue, on Chantilly porcelain in the third quarter of the eighteenth century. The decoration became so popular it was used at Mennecy, Arras, and Tournay and on English porcelain at Derby, Caughley, and elsewhere.

CHINOISERIE. This term is often the cause of confusion. It can only properly be used to mean European decoration done in the Chinese manner with an element of fantasy.

CLOBBERING. The addition of decoration in enamel coloring to Chinese blue-and-white porcelain, mainly by Dutch decorators. Similar work was done on early Worcester wares and by the *Hausmaler* Ferner on Meissen blue-and-white.

COACH POT. An oval or oblong chamber pot used as an article of convenience for travel. Listed in trade lists of English cream-colored earthenware. (See BOURDALOU.)

COPENHAGEN PORCELAIN FACTORY. The royal factory was founded in 1771 with the Queen, Juliane Maria, as the principal shareholder. When financial troubles arose, it was taken over by the King and thenceforward known as Den Kongelige Danske Porcelaen Fabrik. The factory is now one of the world's principal manufacturers of fine porcelain.

CORNUCOPIA. The so-called horn of plenty, from which falls fruit and flowers. In eighteenth-century England especially it was made in both pottery and porcelain for attachment to a wall as a flower vase. Also termed a wall pocket.

CRACKS IN PORCELAIN. These are sometimes called "age cracks," but no porcelain cracks as the result of age. They are either fire cracks or the result of damage, usually the latter. Fire cracks are largely due to faulty design, leading to unequal contraction of parts of the object during cooling or, less often, the unequal distribution of the ingredients in the body.

CRAZING. A fine network of cracks occurring in the glaze of earthenware (sometimes a long time after manufactured) due to the tension set up in the glaze because of unequal shrinkage of glaze and body.

CREIL, OISE, FRANCE. A factory for the manufacture of English-style earthenware was established here *c.* 1794 by an Englishman named Bagnal. It produced white and cream-colored earthenware with views of Paris, portraits of celeb-rities, French châteaux, English country houses, fables of La Fontaine, etc. Mark used was impressed CREIL.

CRYSTALLINE. The term applied by Wedgwood to a class of wares, either surface-painted or of blended colored clays, resembling in hardness, mixture, color, and polish such natural stones as granite, verde antique, red porphyry, ser-pentine, agate, green, jasper, and marble.

DÉCOR BOIS. A form of *trompe-l'oeil* decoration found on eighteenth-century faience and porcelain from France and Germany that imitates a grained wood surface, nearly al-ways with a simulated engraving pinned to it.

DÉJEUNER SET. A porcelain tray, teapot, cream jug, sugar basin, one or two cups, and a porcelain spoon. A set for one person was called a solitaire, for two, a tête-à-tête.

DELLA ROBBIA, ANDREA (1435–1525). A Florentine sculptor, nephew of Luca della Robbia; continued the use of enamelled relief terra-cotta.

DELLA ROBBIA, LUCA (1399–1482). A Florentine sculptor, became celebrated for his works in tin-enamelled terra-cotta.

DIAPER DESIGN. This term should be confined to repetitive patterns of diamond or lozenge shape but is often loosely used for other geometric forms.

DOCCIA PORCELAIN FACTORY. This factory was founded by the Marchese Carlo Ginori in Florence about 1735; it was, however, experimental until ten years later. It is still in existence.

DOULTON, LAMBETH AND BURSLEM. Doulton traded as Doulton & Watts from *c.* 1820 to 1854; then Henry Doulton continued as Doulton & Co. The main productions were utilitarian wares. In 1862, Doulton began experimenting with decorated pottery. The 1871 Exhibition at South Kensington marked the beginning of Doulton's Art Pottery. He employed students from the Lambeth School of Art to decorate the ware. Among the many bodies he produced were salt-glazed stoneware, "Faience," "Impasto," "Silicon," "Carrara," and "Marqueterie" ware, in which various fabrics were impressed into the soft body, giving a woven pattern. Doulton also specialized in architectural terra-cotta work and tiles. In 1882 the manufacture of high-grade porcelain was begun at a separate factory at Burslem. Much Doulton porcelain was produced after 1900 and continues to the present day.

ÉCUELLE. A covered bowl in faience, porcelain, or silver, which was used for the individual service of soup or similar liquid. It consisted of a plain bowl with two horizontally projecting handles and an ornamented cover terminating in a knob of artichoke or similar design. It is a French shape and never became fashionable in England.

EGGSHELL PORCELAIN. Made in China during the Yung-lo period (1403–1424), pared down to such extreme thinness that in the thinnest parts it appeared "bodiless."

ELERS WARE. A generic term for unglazed red stoneware with applied decoration in the style of the Elers brothers, who worked in Staffordshire *c.* 1693 making a redware that is now very rare.

ENCAUSTIC PAINTING. Decoration mainly in red and white on black basalt, invented by Wedgwood in 1769 to imitate the decoration on vases excavated on Italian sites.

ENGINE-TURNING. Decoration produced on the turner's lathe by a species of eccentric chuck. First used by Wedgwood in 1763 for geometric, diced, fluted, and basketwork effects.

EWER. A pitcher or a jug with a wide spout used to carry water for washing hands.

FAÏENCE PATRIOTIQUE. A type of late-eighteenth-century faience decorated with crudely drawn revolutionary subjects, such as the tree of Liberty, the Bastille, etc., and generally with inscriptions like *à la liberté ou à la mort*. Figures usually wear Phrygian caps. Genuine specimens are quite rare; most of those for sale are recent forgeries.

FAMILLE ROSE. A distinctive palette employed in the decoration of Chinese porcelain at the end of the reign of K'ang-hsi (1662–1722).

FERRUGINOUS. Partaking of iron, containing particles of iron.

FINGER VASE. A vase with five flower holders arranged laterally like the thumb and fingers of a hand, commonly made in tin-glazed earthenware. At Vienna five-finger vases were made in porcelain. At Leeds the finger vase was catalogued as a "quintal flower horn." It was also made in Staffordshire.

FLAXMAN, JOHN, R. A. (1755–1826). From 1775 until 1787 he modelled reliefs for Wedgwood's jasper wares, such as the well-known Dancing Hours and Apotheosis of Homer. He exhibited models at the Free Society of Artists in 1767 and 1769, and in 1770 won a silver medal at the Royal Academy.

FLOWN BLUE. An underglaze transfer-printed effect in which the design melts into the surrounding glaze with a kind of colored halo. Caused by firing in an atmosphere containing volatile chlorides. Flown-blue effects were popular in Victorian times. Other colors, such as brown, green, and yellow, are subject to the same treatment but have been little used.

FLUTING. Vertical or spiral channelling, usually semicircular, done on the unfired clay with a tool, by hand, in a mold, or on the engine-turning lathe as devised by Wedgwood in 1763.

FLUX. Any substance or mixture, such as silicates or limestone, used to promote fusion.

FRET. An ornament of straight line or bars arranged in symmetrical patterns.

FRIT. The early factories fused, or fritted, together the fusible ingredients of artificial porcelain to form an amorphous mass, which was then ground to powder and mixed with the clay. For this reason artificial (or soft paste) porcelain is termed "frit porcelain" in some older books.

FUKIEN WARE. Porcelain made during the Ming period in Fukien Province, China; especially a whiteware with ornaments modelled in high relief and applied, termed *blanc de chine*.

FULDA PORCELAIN FACTORY, GERMANY. This factory began with the making of faience in 1741. The first serious attempt to make hard paste porcelain was in 1757. Tablewares and other productions were for the most part copied from Meissen. The mark is either the Fulda coat of arms—a black cross on a white field—or the letters F.D.

GADROON. The unit of a pattern consisting of a series of bold convex curves or loops joined at their ends, common in metalwork and woodwork, frequently used by the potter for the decoration of wares based on silver shapes.

GALLÉ, ÉMILE (1846–1904). Leader of the school that led to a renaissance in the decorative and minor arts, and pioneer in France of Art Nouveau. He drew delicate fancies from the plant world, which he applied to pottery, jewels, etc.

GARNITURE. A term applied to sets of vases used for chimneypiece decoration, usually in porcelain or delft, but also to sets of vases in other materials that sometimes included a central clock. The sets usually consisted of three, five, or even seven alternating covered vases and beakers.

GILES, JAMES (w. 1760–1770). An outside decorator of English porcelain. Much of the best Worcester porcelain of the 1760s came from his studios, but his work may also be found on Chelsea and Bow.

"GIRL-IN-A-SWING" PORCELAIN (c. 1749–1754). At one time attributed to Chelsea, this porcelain is now believed to have been made at a separate factory not far away. It received its name from the first model to be identified. On chemical analysis the porcelain body is very similar to Chelsea triangle wares except that the proportion of lead oxide is much greater.

GLACIER. A vessel of two or more parts for cold desserts, the lower part made to hold ice.

GLOST OVEN. The oven used for firing glazed ware.

GOAT-AND-BEE JUG. A jug decorated in relief with goats and a bee, incised in the base with the word "Chelsea" and a triangle, and sometimes a date, generally 1745, which is regarded as an important documentary piece in respect to the Chelsea factory.

GOTHA PORCELAIN FACTORY. Situated at Gotha in the Thüringerwald, the factory was founded in 1757. The factory continued to operate during the nineteenth century, making porcelain of good quality. Other factories established in 1866 and 1883 are still working today. Gotha is now in East Germany.

GRAIN OF RICE. A decoration produced by perforating the walls of a thin pottery or porcelain vessel and covering it with a translucent glaze that fills the holes and produces an effect something like pearl rice (hence the name).

GRAND FEU. A term for the hottest kiln, used for firing the glaze of hard paste porcelain. Grand feu colors are those that require a high temperature to fire, such as the faience colors, manganese purple, cobalt blue, copper green, antimony yellow, and iron red.

GRIFFIN. A griffin has the head and wings of an eagle (the beak somewhat longer and more sharply hooked) and the body of a lion. It is fairly common in styles founded on classical art and may sometimes be seen during the Empire and Regency periods.

GRISAILLE, EN. Painting in gray monotone in several shades and intensities. Painting *en grisaille* is to be found on porcelain, but the term also refers to *trompe-l'oeil* wall painting of imitation bas-reliefs in stone.

GROG. Pulverized pottery introduced into some pottery bodies to reduce shrinkage during firing.

GROTESQUE. A form of ornament characterized by fantastic shapes based on a combination of human, plant, and animal forms.

HACKWOOD, JOSIAH. A toy- and figure-maker in Upper Hanley during the first half of the nineteenth century. His stock of toys and figures in the biscuit and finished was offered for sale with the models in 1844.

HACKWOOD, WILLIAM (*d.* 1839). A principal modeller to Wedgwood from 1769–1832. He prepared and adapted busts and reliefs from antique sculpture for reproduction in jasper and basalt ware.

HALL, JOHN AND RALPH. Burslem and Tunstall. They made blue-printed earthenware and figures from the early years of the nineteenth century until 1822.

HARLEQUIN. Porcelain fancifully decorated in varied colors. George IV began the widespread vogue for harlequin sets by ordering from the Chamberlain firm at Worcester dinner, dessert, and tea services decorated in the current Japan taste but each piece enamelled with a different design. Other harlequin services were painted with a series of English castles, mansions, or scenic views, each piece displaying one or more different scenes.

HATCHING. A textured background treatment consisting of close parallel lines, or parallel lines crossed at an angle.

HAUSMALEREI. The word means very literally "home painting," and the *Hausmaler* were men and women who obtained wares from the factories and painted them at home or in a studio.

HEATH & SON, BURSLEM, STAFFORDSHIRE. The impressed mark of Heath & Son is thought to be that of a Burslem firm manufacturing white earthenware in the late eighteenth century and early nineteenth.

HEATHCOTE, C., AND CO., LONGTON. Made good-quality blue-printed earthenware (sometimes from Turner's engravings) as well as painted and gilded wares; early nineteenth century. The mark consisted of Prince of Wales feathers with the name "C. Heathcote & Co." in an arc above.

HENSHALL & WILLIAMSON, LONGPORT. Successors to William Clowers & Co., earthenware manufacturers and makers of black basalt, Longport, Burslem, from *c.* 1800. The partnership dissolved in 1830.

HERCULANEUM (LIVERPOOL) POTTERY. Started in 1794 producing similar wares to Staffordshire—creamware, pearlware, basalt, lustered earthenware, and terra-cotta. After 1800 there was a limited production of porcelain. The factory-flourished between 1806 and 1833, and closed in 1841. Articles most obtainable were creamware, blue-painted, transfer-printed, and very occasionally polychrome. Jugs of creamware transfer-printed in black are the most sought-after, especially those with named ships forming part of the decoration. Much of the early production was unmarked, but "Herculaneum" impressed and printed is found on some early wares. After 1822 they are marked "Herculaneum" pottery. The Liverbird is a late mark used after 1833.

HICKS & MEIGH, SHELTON, STAFFORDSHIRE. Successors to the Baddeleys of Shelton and manufacturers of good ironstone china from 1810 to 1835. Transfer-printed and enamelled ware were manufactured.

HILDITCH, LANE END. The firm of Hilditch .& Co. made bone china from about 1805 until 1813, when partners and name changed, and continued until 1867. The mark H & S within a wreath and underneath a crown or within a square frame beneath an eagle were used.

HIPPOCAMPUS. A legendary water animal with the body and fore-legs of a horse and a dolphin's tail.

"HOB-IN-THE-WELL" PATTERN. A Japanese Imari pattern in the so-called Kakiemon style that depicts a mythical incident in the boyhood of a Chinese sage who saved his young companion from drowning in a fish bowl by throwing a stone at it and breaking it.

HOMERIC VASE. Regarded by Wedgwood as his greatest achievement other than the Portland vase. The cameo subject, "The Apotheosis of Homer," was modelled by Flaxman, *c.* 1776.

HUDIBRAS. An equestrian figure made by Ralph Wood of Burslem after an engraving by William Hogarth for an illustrated edition of Butler's *Satire* published in 1726. Popular over a long period and made in earthenware with glazed colors and enamel effects from 1770 until 1800.

IMAGES, IMAGE TOYS. Earthenware, stoneware, or porcelain miniature figures. The word occurs in an advertisement of William Littler & Co.

IMARI PORCELAIN. Japanese porcelain with painted decoration based on textile patterns was called Imari after the port it was shipped from. Imari was in the province of Hizen, not far from Arita, where the porcelain was made and decorated. It has an overcrowded pattern painted in a number of colors, of which a blackish dark blue and a strong dark red predominate. It was first made a little after 1700, probably at the suggestion of Dutch merchants. The earliest specimens were well painted, but quality deteriorated as the eighteenth century progressed. By far the greater numbers of examples to be found today were made in the nineteenth century, when quality was extremely poor. The decoration was copied in China at the beginning of the eighteenth century, and also in Europe, especially at the Worcester factory. (See JAPAN DECORATION.)

INDIAN CHINA. All porcelain imported by the English from the East, mainly from Japan and China.

INDIANISCHE BLUMEN. Formal oriental flowers, a common decoration of Meissen and other porcelain from 1725.

INTAGLIO. A form of incised ornament in which the design is sunk below the surface. Seals are often cut in this way, and molds for bas-reliefs are similar.

JACKFIELD POTTERY, SHROPSHIRE. The principal ware made at the pottery at Jackfield from 1750 to 1775 seems to have been a red earthenware body covered with a black glaze that was decorated with oil gilding and oil or lacquer painting.

JAPAN DECORATION. A European decoration on porcelain and pottery in the Japanese style of Imari or Kakiemon. Such motifs as the dragon, phoenix, peony, and chrysanthemum were used in rust reds and cobalt blue, among other colors.

JARDINIERE. A stand for flowers and plants made of wood, porcelain, faience, or metal.

JASPER DIP. Colored solution applied to a white jasper body by dipping; also white jasper covered with a surface coloring.

JESUIT CHINA. Porcelain exported from China as early as 1740 and inspired by drawings and engravings taken to China by missionaries or traders. They were usually pencil drawings, and an attempt was occasionally made to lighten the gray or black lines with touches of gold and later with flesh tones on hands and faces. Many of the subjects were religious, and some were mythological or genre.

JET-ENAMELLED WARE. One of the most celebrated productions of the Worcester porcelain factory in the eighteenth century, consisting of wares transfer-printed in black. James Giles, an enameller, purchased "jet-enamelled services" from Worcester in 1769.

JEWELLED PORCELAIN. Although precious stones, such as turquoises, were occasionally inset into Böttger's red stoneware, the term is usually used to refer to a type of decoration invented about 1781 at Sèvres by Cotteau, in which drops of translucent enamel were applied over gold foil. A similar process was in use in Germany, and it was revived at Worcester in 1865 for a service made for the Countess of Dudley.

KAKIEMON. The family name of Japanese porcelain decorators. The designs of the best period, between 1680 and 1720, are asymmetrical, leaving empty spaces. The distinctive palette includes iron red, a bluish green, light blue, and yellow. These designs were copied by Meissen, Chantilly, and Chelsea. The Quail pattern is a well-known example.

KAOLIN. The Chinese name (*kao-ling*) for the fine white clay necessary for making true porcelain. It is formed by the decomposition of feldspathic rock. In England it is called China clay.

KAUFFMANN, ANGELICA (1741–1807). A Swiss painter who was in London from 1766 until 1781. She was a friend of Reynolds' and a founder of the Royal Academy in 1768. She designed and painted panels for the Adam brothers, although most work in her style was not from her hand and examples actually painted by her are very rare. Vienna and other Continental porcelain plates of the nineteenth century signed "Angelica Kauffmann" are not hers.

KNOP. A knob, such as that forming the handle of an eighteenth-century teapot lid, which took various ornamental forms—a flower, a fir cone, a pineapple, or an artichoke.

KRATER. From the Greek verb "to mix." A wide-mouthed jar or deep bowl with two horizontal vertical loop handles, used for mixing wine and water.

KUTANI. Japanese porcelain made *c.* 1650–1750 in Kaga Province. Average-quality body but good decoration, using an intense blue, green, yellow, and purple.

KWAART. The transparent lead overglaze applied after it had been painted in color to the tin-enamelled earthenware made at Delft, Holland.

KYLIN. A mythical animal with the head of a dragon, the body of a lion, and the feet of a deer.

KYLIX. A drinking cup in the form of a shallow bowl on a stem that is often tall. Usually it had two horizontal handles: a *tazza*, or stem cup.

LACEWORK. In porcelain this form was introduced before 1770 at Meissen. Actual lace was dipped into porcelain slip (body diluted with water to the consistency of cream) and applied to the figure. The lace burned away in the kiln, leaving its image in porcelain.

LAKIN & POOLE, BURSLEM, STAFFORDSHIRE. These two entered into partnership in 1791, and with changes in partnership continued until 1797, when the works became bankrupt. Their mark is impressed LAKIN & POOLE.

LAMBREQUINS. A type of ornament most commonly seen on early eighteenth-century Rouen faience and on early porcelain from Saint-Cloud. It is an abstract ornament based on pendent lacework, scrollwork, and the decoration of bookcovers. The origin of this pattern was the engraved designs of Jean Bérain.

LANGE LYZEN. Dutch: "Long Elizas." Figures of women copied from Chinese porcelain by European faience and porcelain painters (nearly always in blue), in which height and slenderness have been exaggerated. They can be seen quite often decorating early Worcester blue-and-white porcelain.

The prototypes are to be found on Chinese porcelain exported during the reign of Wan-li (1573–1619).

LAZULITE. A blue-tinted Parian ware.

LESSORE, ÉMILE (*d.* 1876). Porcelain painter at Sèvres until 1850, when he set up in Paris. In 1858 he went to England and worked for Wedgwood at Etruria. Lessore decorated pottery with scenes of rustic sentiment in an impressionistic, broken touch.

LITHOGRAPHY. A process for reproducing pictorial effects, in color or monochrome, invented about 1796, using the grease-holding and water-repelling properties of oölitic limestone.

LITHOPHANES. Flat plaques of thin biscuit porcelain with molded intaglio decoration intended to be viewed only by transmitted light. They were first made about 1830 and continued to be produced until about 1900. The best were made by Continental factories, especially the German ones.

LUNÉVILLE FAIENCE. This factory was founded in 1758. It is known that it was making creamware as early as 1765, because some specimens are in the rococo style.

LUSTERS. Vases with prismatic glass pendants.

MAASTRICHT, HOLLAND. A large industrial pottery called De Sphinx was established in Maastricht by Petrus Regort in 1836 and was extensively developed in the second half of the nineteenth century. In 1899 about eighteen hundred workers were employed. Transfer-printed tea and dinner services were made in ironstone china.

MADELEY, SHROPSHIRE. A factory for the manufacture of soft paste porcelain is said to have been established at Madeley about 1826 by a potter who had previously worked at Coalport, T. M. Randall.

"MAJOLICA." A nineteenth-century earthenware covered with brightly colored lead glazes introduced at Wedgwood works in 1860 and made by many other potters. The name was derived from the entirely different low-fired earthenware covered with white, opaque, tin enamel made in Italy during the Renaissance.

MANGANESE PURPLE. A basic stain for ceramic glazes and bodies and an important color for use in decoration.

MARBLED WARE. Earthenware veined and mottled by sponging or combing together different colored slips.

MARIEBERG PORCELAIN FACTORY, SWEDEN. The manufacture of porcelain at the Marieberg factory was a later extension of the faience undertaking begun in 1759. A soft paste porcelain was produced by 1766, and by 1788 the factory was producing a hard paste ware. The porcelain of Marieberg is rare. The two principal influences were Mennecy in the early period and Copenhagen in the later.

MASK. The human face in mask form. A popular ornament from early Renaissance times onward. The mask took many forms—Medusa heads, satyrs, and grotesques with distorted features, often in conjunction with foliage. A molded design when found on pottery and porcelain.

MAZARINE BLUE. The English name given to the intense blue introduced at Chelsea and other factories, imitating the splendid *gros bleu* of Vincennes.

MOCHA WARE. A form of "dipped" pottery decorated with colored bands into which tree, moss, or fernlike effects have been introduced by means of a diffusing agent, a drop of which spreads the colored bands to produce the pattern.

MONKEY (OR APE) ORCHESTRA. A series of twenty-one porcelain figures of monkeys playing instruments with a conductor.

First modelled by Kändler at Meissen in 1747. They were copied at other factories—Vienna, Fürstenberg, Chelsea, Derby, etc.—and reproduced extensively in the nineteenth century.

MONOCHROME. A painting or drawing in a single hue.

MOUSTIERS. Moustiers (1679–1874) was one of the most important faience centers of France. Several factories operated here, making various types of pottery in many forms.

MUFFLE KILN. An oven used inside a furnace in firing wares that must be protected from flame.

NAPLES PORCELAIN FACTORY (THE ROYAL). Started in 1771 by Ferdinand IV in an attempt to revive the earlier porcelain of Capo di Monte, and there is some resemblance. The factory was sold in 1806 to a French company. The mark was an N surmounted by a crown. The factory later had various private owners and closed in 1834. The mark of the crown and N is copied on many French and German late-nineteenth and twentieth-century articles and fraudulently sold for Capo di Monte.

NEREID. A sea nymph, usually to be found with a triton, sometimes the subject of porcelain figures during the rococo period.

NIDERVILLER FAIENCE AND PORCELAIN FACTORY, MOSELLE, FRANCE. The faience factory was founded in 1754. The products were finely executed, the early wares very similar to Strassburg. Porcelain making began about 1756. The factory is still in existence.

OEIL DE PERDRIX. Literally, "eye of a partridge." A diaper of small circles in gold used to enrich colored grounds or to subdue their strong tones.

ONION PATTERN. An extremely popular design introduced at the

Meissen factory by J. G. Höroldt about 1735 and still in use in one or another of its many variants at other factories today. It does not represent onion flowers, but the fruits, blossoms, and foliage of asters and peonies, adapted from a Chinese original.

ORMOLU. Literally means gilding with gold paste. Refers to gilding bronze with an amalgam of mercury and gold which, when combined, form a pasty mass. In England "ormolu" is also used to denote an alloy similar to brass of a light golden color. Used in mounts for porcelains.

PALISSY, BERNARD (1510–1590). He became a potter in 1540 and after pursuing many experiments began to produce his rustic wares—large dishes, usually oval, with a yellowish-white clay body, the reverse covered with a mottled glaze similar to tortoise shell. Decoration was with colored lead glazes using only a few simple colors—cobalt blue, copper green, manganese violet, and yellow. The center of the dish was painted with a stream of water in and around which are reptiles, plants, shells, insects, and similar natural objects modelled in relief, some obviously cast from life. Palissy's ware was very popular with collectors in the nineteenth century, when it brought high prices. Consequently, forgeries and reproductions are numerous.

PÂTE-SUR-PÂTE. This means, literally, "paste on paste." The technique is essentially painting designs on the unfired, unglazed body of porcelain in liquid white slip. It was first employed in Europe at Sèvres soon after 1850. It had been used by the Chinese in the eighteenth century. It was perfected by Marc-Louis Solon, who did work for Minton that was much sought after. It was also used by the Rookwood Pottery of Cincinnati.

PETIT (JACOB ET MARDOCHÉE) PORCELAIN FACTORY. Established at Fontainebleau in 1795 and bought by J. & M. Petit *c.*

1830. Much decorative porcelain was made here, mostly in early-nineteenth-century styles. It specialized in figures. Some clockcases surmounted by figures are very large and well painted. The initials J.P. are used as a mark.

PILLEMENT, JEAN-BAPTISTE (1728–1803). French designer of ornament, born in Lyon. His designs were principally in the rococo style, and chiefly *chinoiseries* and *singeries*. They occur on porcelain from several factories, and on faience and enamels. Pillement painted landscapes in the manner of Boucher.

PINXTON, DERBYSHIRE. A small porcelain factory (1796–1812) working principally in the Derby tradition, founded by William Billingsley. Production was small and specimens are rare. Decoration was principally flowers, but occasionally landscapes.

PLASTER OF PARIS. Calcined gypsum in white, powdery form, used as a material for making fine and ornamental casts; characterized by its ability to set rapidly when mixed with water.

"POMPEIAN SCROLL." A neoclassical decoration combining light, graceful scrollwork, grotesques, and *putti*, derived from the frescoes of Pompeii. Used extensively at Sèvres and at Paris porcelain factories from 1780. Similar decorations were used at Vienna and Meissen.

PORTLAND VASE, THE. The Portland vase (also known as the Barberini vase), which is now in the British Museum, is the finest example of Roman cameo glass known to survive. The Dowager Duchess of Portland acquired it in 1784, and after her death her son lent it to Josiah Wedgwood to copy in 1785, which he did, in jasper. The first Wedgwood edition, of which about sixteen survive, was issued in 1790, but there have been several subsequent editions.

POWDER BLUE. The name is derived from the Chinese technique of blowing powdered pigment through a bamboo tube with fine gauze stretched across its aperture. This technique was adopted at Meissen, Bow, Worcester, Caughley, and American art manufacturers.

PRESS MOLDS. Molds of fire clay or plaster of Paris used in the manufacture of pottery and porcelain, especially of porcelain flowers. The porcelain body, while plastic, is pressed into the molds.

PROOF CONDITION. Perfect, no damages or repairs.

PUTTI. Also termed *amorini*, figures of Cupid, or winged cupid's heads, often used as decoration and often occurring on porcelain.

QUIMPER (LOC MARIA) FAIENCE. In Brittany the factory of Quimper was second only to those at Rennes. It was founded in 1690. Faience is still being made at Quimper.

RAUENSTEIN PORCELAIN FACTORY. This Thuringian factory was founded in 1783. For the most part, production consisted of inferior copies of Meissen with a grayish glaze. Porcelain was made here during the nineteenth century as well, bearing a mark intended to simulate the crossed swords of Meissen with the addition of R-n, the eighteenth-century mark.

"REBEKAH-AT-THE-WELL" TEAPOT. Originated and first made in Rockingham ware by Edwin Bennett, Baltimore, of E. & W. Bennett pottery, in 1851, and continued for many years. The pattern was so popular that nearly all other American potteries copied it. On opposite sides of the vessel is a figure in relief of a maiden with water jar, resting or standing by a well, and beneath are the words "Rebekah at the Well."

REIGN MARKS. Marks consisting of four or six characters, which are to be found on many kinds of Chinese decorative art, and commonly on porcelain. The full six-character mark gives the dynasty and the Emperor's name, and they read from the right and downward.

RENNES FAIENCE, BRITTANY. The first-known factory here started in 1748. Surviving faience from Rennes is difficult to attribute. Wares were influenced by Rouen, Moustiers, and Marseille.

RESERVE. A space—oval, round, or rectangular—on a surface retained for a different decoration, usually scenes, flowers, or fruits.

RETICULATED. An article that is pierced or netted.

ROSE POMPADOUR. A ground color introduced at Sèvres porcelain factory in 1759. It was discontinued after the death of Madame de Pompadour in 1764. Rose Pompadour is a rose pink related to the purple of Cassius and the Chinese *famille rose*. A version of it was employed in England during the nineteenth century under the misnomer rose du Barry.

ROSSO ANTICO. As the name implies, an imitation of the red pottery of Greece and Rome. It was Wedgwood's version of red stoneware. The body was very similar to black basalt, and it is sometimes found decorated with black figures in imitation of Greek black figure vases.

ROUEN FAIENCE AND PORCELAIN, NORMANDY, FRANCE. This capital city of Normandy produced faience from the middle sixteenth century until the late seventeenth century. Blue-and-white was dominant, but the colors green, yellow, and red were gradually added. Louis Poterat applied for the privilege to make porcelain in 1673, but only a few specimens have been attributed to Rouen.

ROUNDEL. A round decorative panel or plaque.

SAGGER. A fire-clay box in which earthenware is placed when being fired in the oven.

SAMSON, EDMÉ, ET CIE, PARIS. A name that soon becomes very familiar to the collector of old pottery and porcelain. Samson produced almost every variety, and copies of their products are often presented in the shops of less knowledgeable dealers as originals. The firm was founded in 1845 and is credited with far more than it actually made. The name has become almost a generic term for a clever reproduction. Samson also made reproductions of Battersea, Bilston, and Birmingham enamel.

SANG DE BOEUF. A blood-red *flambé* glaze copied from the Chinese in the latter part of the nineteenth century.

SATYR. A woodland deity in human form, either with horse's ears and tail or with goat's ears. A molded satyr mask was a popular subject for Staffordshire pottery jugs in the second half of the eighteenth century. Mask spouts occur on jugs modelled of overlapping leaves made *c.* 1760 at Worcester.

SAXE, PORCELAINE DE. Just as the English have always mistakenly called Meissen porcelain "Dresden," so the French have referred to it as "Saxe" (Saxon).

SCHWARZLOT. Painting done in black monochrome on porcelain, faience, and glass in a style usually inspired by line engravings. Work of this kind is found frequently on German porcelain of the first half of the eighteenth century and is more often than not the work of one of the *Hausmaler*.

SGRAFFITO. Literally, "scratched." When applied to pottery, it means ware that has been washed over with a slip of a different color than the body; then the decoration is incised, through the overwash.

SINGERIES. Models of monkeys in mocking or fantastic attitudes. The vogue for *singeries* was extensive in the baroque and early rococo phases of porcelain manufacture.

"SNOWMAN" FIGURES. Porcelain figures covered with a thick, opaque glaze obscuring the modelling. They are early productions of William Littler of Longton Hall.

SOAPSTONE (STEATITE OR TALC). A magnesium silicate. The stone has a greasy feel and is easily carved. It was extensively used for small ornaments by the Chinese; less frequently in Europe. Crushed soapstone replaces feldspar in some eighteenth-century English porcelains, notably those of Worcester.

SOLITAIRE SET. A tea or coffee set for one person.

SOLON, MARC-EMMANUEL (1835–1912). A French modeller and decorator who developed the technique of *pâte-sur-pâte*, or *pâte d'application*, at the Sèvres factory, where he worked from 1862 until 1871, when he went to England and worked at Minton in Stoke-on-Trent.

"SPA" CUPS. Special cups decorated with views of spa towns made by the Bohemian porcelain factories for those partaking of the waters.

SPONGED WARE. A crude, easily recognized peasant style of decoration achieved by free painting or by dabbing the ware with a sponge impregnated with pigment.

SPUR MARKS. Rough marks formed by the spurs or stilts on which the glazed wares rest in the oven during the firing process.

STANDISH. An inkstand.

STANNIFEROUS FAIENCE. Tin-enamelled or tin-glazed earthenware made extensively in Europe.

STEATITE. Also termed soapstone.

SWAG. A suspended festoon of foliage, fruit, flowers, or drapery of classical origin, very popular among such neoclassical designers as the Adam brothers.

TASSIE, JAMES (1735–1799). Producer of replicas of ancient engraved gems from a glass paste he made from finely powdered glass. He supplied molds of cameos and intaglios to Wedgwood for reproduction in the latter's basalt bodies. His fame as a maker of plaster molds was sufficient to cause him to be commissioned to take the first casts of the Portland vase.

TEBO, MR. (c. 1760). An itinerant porcelain modeller.

TERRA-COTTAS. Unglazed objects made from natural ferruginous clay. These vary in color after firing from brick red to buff. Terra-cottas vary in hardness according to firing temperature, but most are comparatively soft. They are often painted.

TÊTE-À-TÊTE, OR DÉJEUNER. A tea or coffee set for two, with an oval serving tray or plate with ears, two cups and saucers, teapot, coffeepot, and sugar basin.

TIGER WARE (OR TYGER WARE). A sixteenth-century English term for stoneware jugs imported from the Rhineland that have a mottled brown glaze.

TORTOISE-SHELL WARE. A term sometimes applied to the earthenware of Thomas Whieldon and others that was covered with mottled-colored lead glazes, usually manganese-brown with touches of blue.

TREMBLEUSE SAUCER. A saucer with a raised ring around the

well, or a very deeply sunk well, to form a receptacle for the cup. Suitable for aged people with trembling hands or for people sick in bed.

TRITON. Mythological son of Poseidon and Amphitrite who has the head and trunk of a man and the tail of a fish and uses a conch shell as a trumpet.

TROMPE-L'OEIL. The painting of motifs or objects in such a way that they may be mistaken for the real thing: deceptive realism.

TROPHIES. Decorative arrangements of weapons, armor, tools, utensils, and musical instruments employed on ceramics.

UNAKER. Virginia china clay. The substance played an influential part in the development of the porcelain industry in England. This Cherokee clay was imported by Wedgwood for use in making his jasper wares.

VEILLEUSE. Literally "night lamp." The *veilleuse* is a tea or food warmer. They are found in earthenware, stoneware, and porcelain, some in tin-enamelled ware. The date of origin is about the middle of the eighteenth century, and they were made in most countries. In general they consist of a base on which is placed a cylindrical chimney pierced toward the top to allow hot air to escape, surmounted by a covered food container at first, and later by a teapot. The chimney has an aperture at the bottom to allow for the insertion of a lamp, the *godet,* which is a small cup containing oil with a floating wick.

VERMICULÉ GROUNDS. An irregular tracery pattern of meandering wriggling lines breaking up a ground color into islands, executed in gold or in color over another color, giving a marbled effect.

VILLEROY AND BOCH. The firm was founded in 1841 by the families of Villeroy and Boch to amalgamate the resources of the pottery factories at Wallerfängen, Septfontaines, and Mettlach. The output of these combined factories, including one built in Dresden in 1853, covered almost every field of ornamental and useful pottery. In 1899, six thousand people were employed.

VOLSTEDT PORCELAIN FACTORY. Established in Thuringia, Germany, about 1760. It continues today under the name Alteste Volkstedte. The crossed hayforks from the Schwarzburg arms with a line across have been used as a mark since 1787.

WASTERS (KILN). Wares that become defective in the kiln either because of overfiring, which may make them collapse or come out of true, or through the running of a glaze, causing them to stick to the sagger or to another article. Wasters often throw light on technical methods and when found on excavation sites have considerable documentary and historical value.

WATTEAU, JEAN ANTOINE (1684–1721). A French artist who painted subjects derived from Italian or French comedy. The make-believe world and the tender amorousness of his subjects appealed strongly to later generations, and they were perpetuated with variations on porcelain at many factories in the eighteenth century.

WHEEL-ENGRAVING. Engraving on the lapidary's wheel as practiced at Meissen on Böttger's red stoneware.

YING-CH'ING. A beautiful, thin translucent Chinese porcelain with a granular, sugary body and pale-bluish glaze. A recent term.

ZAFFER. Term current among eighteenth-century English potters for cobalt blue used for painting underglaze. The word was derived from the Italian *qaffare*, meaning cobalt in the form of glass frit obtained from Venice. This was finely powdered and used as a pigment.

Bibliography and Index

Bibliography

GENERAL

Chaffers, William. *Marks and Monograms on European and Oriental Pottery and Porcelain.* 14th Revised Edition. Los Angeles: Borden, 1946.

Cushion, J. P. *Pocket Book of English Ceramic Marks.* London: Faber and Faber, 1959.

Eberlein, Harold Donaldson, and Roger Wearne Ramsdell. *The Practical Book of Chinaware.* New York: Halcyon House, 1925.

Godden, Geoffrey A. *Encyclopedia of British Pottery and Porcelain Marks.* New York: Crown, 1964.

————. An *Illustrated Encyclopedia of British Pottery and Porcelain*. New York: Crown, 1966.

Haggar, Reginald G. *The Concise Encyclopedia of Continental Pottery and Porcelain*. New York: Hawthorn, 1960.

Mankowitz, Wolf, and Reginald G. Haggar. *The Concise Encyclopedia of English Pottery and Porcelain*. New York: Hawthorn, 1957.

Savage, George. *Dictionary of Antiques*. New York: Praeger, 1970.

CHINESE

Frank, Ann. *Chinese Blue and White*. New York: Walker, 1969.

Garner, Sir Harry Mason. *Oriental Blue and White*. New York: Praeger, 1971.

Jenyns, Soame. *Later Chinese Porcelain: The Ch'ing Dynasty: 1644–1912*. London: Faber and Faber, 1965.

CHINESE EXPORT

Beurdeley, Michel. *Chinese Trade Porcelain*. Rutland, Vt.: Charles E. Tuttle, 1962.

Crossman, Carl L. *A Design Catalogue of Chinese Export Porcelain for the American Market*. Salem, Mass.: Peabody Museum, 1964.

Farnham, Katharine Gross, and Callie Huger Efird. *Chinese Export Porcelain from the Reeves Collection*. A catalogue of a loan exhibition held at the High Museum of Art, Atlanta, Georgia, 1969.

Gordon, Horace W., and Elinor Gordon. *Oriental Lowestoft (Chinese Export Porcelain)*. Published by Elinor Gordon, 1959.

Hyde, J. A. Loyde. *Oriental Lowestoft, Chinese Export Porcelain, Porcelaine de la Cie des Indes*. Newport, Monmouthshire: The Ceramic Book Co., 1954.

Tin-Glazed Earthenware

Jonge, C. H. de. *Delft Ceramics.* New York: Praeger, 1970.
Moore, N. Hudson. *Delftware Dutch and English.* New York:
F. A. Stokes Co., 1908.

Continental

Honey, W. B. *Dresden China.* New York: Tudor, 1946.
———. *French Porcelain of the Eighteenth Century.* New York:
Pitman, n.d.
Plinval de Guillebon, Régine de. *Porcelain of Paris, 1770–1850.*
New York: Walker, 1972.
Savage, George. *Eighteenth Century German Porcelain.*
London: Spring Books, 1950.

English Porcelain

Bedford, John. *Old Worcester Porcelain.* New York: Walker,
1966.
Fisher, Stanley W. *The Decoration of English Porcelain.* London: Derek Verschoyle, 1954.
———. *English Blue and White Porcelain of the 18th Century.*
London: Batsford, 1947.
Gilhespy, F. Brayshaw. *Derby Porcelain.* London: Spring Books,
1961.
Godden, Geoffrey A. *Caughley and Worcester Porcelains, 1775–
1800.* New York: Praeger, 1969.
———. *Coalport and Coalbrookdale Porcelains.* New York:
Praeger, 1970.
———. *The Illustrated Guide to Lowestoft Porcelain.* New
York: Praeger, 1969.
———. *Minton Pottery and Porcelain of the First Period, 1793–
1850.* New York: York: Praeger, 1968.

Hackenbroch, Yvonne. *Chelsea and Other English Porcelain.* The Metropolitan Museum of Art/Harvard University Press, 1957.

Hayden, Arthur. *Chats on English China.* London: T. Fisher Unwin, 1920.

Hurlbutt, Frank. *Old Derby Porcelain and Its Artist-Workmen.* New York: Frederick A. Stokes Co., 1925.

Sandon, Henry. *The Illustrated Guide to Worcester Porcelain, 1751–1793.* New York: Praeger, 1970.

Savage, George. *Eighteenth Century English Porcelain.* London: Spring Books, 1952.

Stringer, George Eyre. *New Hall Porcelain.* London: The Art Trade Press, 1949.

Watney, Dr. Bernard. *English Blue and White Porcelain of the 18th Century.* London: Faber and Faber, 1963.

———. *Longton Hall Porcelain.* London: Faber and Faber, 1957.

English Pottery

Camehl, Ada Walker. *The Blue China Book.* New York: Halcyon House, 1916.

Earle, Mrs. Alice Morse. *China Collecting in America.* New York: Scribner's, 1892.

Godden, Geoffrey A. *The Illustrated Guide to Mason's Patent Ironstone China.* New York: Praeger, 1971.

Gorely, Jean. *Wedgwood.* New York: Gramercy, 1950.

Hayden, Arthur. *Chats on English Earthenware.* London: T. Fisher Unwin, 1900.

Hughes, G. Bernard. *English Pottery and Porcelain Figures.* New York: Praeger, 1968.

———. *Victorian Pottery and Porcelain.* London: Spring Books, 1959.

Little, W. L. *Staffordshire Blue.* New York: Crown, 1969.

McCauley, Robert H. *Liverpool Transfer Designs on Anglo-American Pottery.* Portland, Me.: The Southworth-Anthoensen Press, 1942.

Mankowitz, Wolf. *Wedgwood.* London: Batsford, 1953.

Meteyard, Eliza. *Wedgwood and His Works.* London: Bell and Daldy, 1873.

Towner, Donald C. *The Leeds Pottery.* New York: Taplinger, 1965.

Whiter, Leonard R. *Spode: A History of the Family Factory and Wares from 1733–1833.* New York: Praeger, 1971.

Williams, Sydney B. *Antique Blue and White Spode.* London: Batsford, 1943.

AMERICAN

Barber, Dr. Edwin A. *The Pottery and Porcelain of the United States.* New York–London: Putnam, 1893.

Barret, Richard Carter. *Bennington Pottery and Porcelain.* New York: Bonanza Books, 1958.

Henzke, Lucile. *American Art Pottery.* Camden, N.Y.: Thomas Nelson, 1970.

Peck, Herbert. *The Book of Rookwood Pottery.* New York: Bonanza Books, 1968.

Ramsey, John. *American Potters and Pottery.* New York: Tudor, 1947.

Spargo, John. *Potters and Potteries of Bennington.* New York: Houghton, 1926.

Tucker China: 1825–1838. Catalogue of an exhibition at the Philadelphia Museum of Art, May 4 through September 9, 1957.

Index

A Note on the Type

The text of this book was set in Electra, a Linotype face designed by W. A. Dwiggins (1880–1956), who was responsible for so much that is good in contemporary book design. Although much of his early work was in advertising and he was the author of the standard volume *Layout in Advertising*, Mr. Dwiggins later devoted his prolific talents to book typography and type design and worked with great distinction in both fields. In addition to his designs for Electra, he created the Metro, Caledonia, and Eldorado series of type faces, as well as a number of experimental cuttings that have never been issued commercially.

Electra cannot be classified as either modern or old-style. It is not based on any historical model, nor does it echo a particular period or style. It avoids the extreme contrast between thick and thin elements that marks most modern faces and attempts to give a feeling of fluidity, power, and speed.

This book was composed by The Haddon Craftsmen, Inc., Scranton, Pennsylvania; and was printed and bound by Halliday Lithograph Corporation, West Hanover, Massachusetts.

The book was designed by Earl Tidwell.